A MONOGRAPH.

A NEW THEORY AND PRACTICE IN TEACHING.

BY

R. D. ALLEN and J. T. GAINES.

ERRATA.

At bottom of page 23 read "8_t^1" for "8^1."

In Prin. 16, page 25, for "b^1" read "a^1."

LOUISVILLE:
PUBLISHED BY J. T. GAINES
1889

A MONOGRAPH.

A New Theory and Practice in Teaching.

BY

R. D. ALLEN and J. T. GAINES.

LOUISVILLE:
PUBLISHED BY J. T. GAINES
1889

PREFACE.

The authors believe that in this little volume they have presented something new on the subject of education.

Associated in normal school work in the summer of 1878, they first exchanged views upon the art of teaching. Beginning with substantial agreement in theory and in methods, each has ever found profit and pleasure in hearing the experiences of the other in, to him, a strange field of labor—the one being in the public school work, and the other in charge of a select private school for boys.

The fact observed by both, that a method devised for use in one field could be successfully applied in the other, suggested the possibility of systematizing all teaching.

Frequent consultations and exchanges of experiences with this end in view have taken place. Many things have transpired to delay the accomplishment of their plans. They do not now claim to have discovered all or to have devised a perfect system. But some principles are now clear that were once dark; others are growing clearer as experiment burnishes them. Enough has been completed to justify submitting their views to the great brotherhood of teachers.

They ask for and ardently desire criticism, both favorable and adverse; the Empire would not have been had no enemies opposed Napoleon, nor would the Lieutenant have been the Emperor had no friends upheld him.

The chief concern of the authors has been to be understood. Pestalozzi, Froebel, and Horace Mann were not understood by their cotemporaries, nor is Parker fully understood to-day. And why? *No one can learn a fact by reading it or by hearing it unless he knows it already in its elements.* It is by the light of our experience as teachers that we must read the words of a brother. Practical lessons are given within these pages. Begin by trying these, and with the light they shed seek to know the truths contained herein. That they are valuable may well be claimed, for they are the assimilations from observations and comparisons upon more than twenty years of active school-room work.

The postulates for teaching, on page 17 and following, were first noted down as inductions from observations of work in teaching. After they were agreed upon, a theory was sought that would satisfy them. That theory has been found, and it is the mission of this Monograph to expound it. It is believed that it will satisfy all experiences, from that of the mother-teacher to that of the university professor; that it will meet the wants of all grades and kinds of teaching.

No such absurd claim is set up as that there has been no effective teaching heretofore; it is only asserted that often where good teaching has been done it has resulted from pursuing the line of least resistance, and has not been dictated by principle.

It is a fact, which no one can deny, that the majority of teachers do adhere to definitions and make them the basis for their work.

Believing it to be true, that there is not a principle or truth to be found in any department of knowledge which can not be so presented that the pupil shall himself discover it, the authors submit the result of their labors to their colleagues in the hope that many who are now working in darkness may thereafter walk in the light.

Thanks are due to Prof. F. E. Spaulding, of Louisville Military Academy, to Hiram Roberts, of the Louisville Training School, and to Messrs. Wm. J. McConathy, Wm. Marriner, W. O. Cross, and O. B. Theiss, of the Public Schools of Louisville, for valuable suggestions.

R. D. ALLEN,
J. T. GAINES.

LOUISVILLE, KY., November, 1889.

THEORY.

The practice of teaching set forth in this Monograph is based on the theory that "The primary attributes of intellect are, (1) Consciousness of Differences; (2) Consciousness of Agreement, and (3) Retentiveness. Every properly intellectual function involves one or more of these attributes, and nothing else." [Bain's Mental Science.]

If it appears that Abstraction, Judgment, Reason, Memory, and Imagination,* the so-called faculties of the Intellect, can be adequately explained on this theory, then it must be evident that a correct practice in teaching must ever engage the powers of the intellect in "Differences," in "Agreements," and in "Retentiveness," and also that any practice in teaching which is not founded on the three attributes mentioned is wrong, and therefore injurious in proportion to its departure from these essentials to all healthful activities of the intellect.

No one can question the proposition that agreement of objects in qualities is the foundation of all classification. This action of the intellect (originating classes) is called *Abstraction* by some; by others it is called the *Notion-forming Power*.

Observe the mind at work assigning an object to a class already formed. Does the intellect not discover the resemblance or agreement of the object with the notion, which is the basis for the class? Is not this *Judgment?*

If an intellect, without bringing two objects, A and B, in conjunction, perceives their agreement by virtue of perceived

---

*Intellectual Consciousness and Sense have not been included in this analysis of the faculties, as some prefer, because they are conceived to be merely the acts of intellect in separating objects internal and external. In either case, if the classification be retained, the act named by the term is better expressed by the first attribute—Consciousness of Differences.

resemblances in each to C, with which it in turn has been compared, and again discovers agreement in D and E by virtue of resemblances in each to F, and thus continues multiplying its experiences, will it not at length perceive the agreement in these experiences and be able to arrive at the law: "In so far as two things resemble a third they resemble each other?" And is not this an exercise of the intellect in that mode of its existence called *Reason?* And is any thing else involved in the whole process, except agreements, differences, and retentiveness?

In all these acts, in abstraction, in judgment, and in reason, does not the *Memory* repeatedly exhibit itself? What is memory if it be not a recurrence of a preceding state of the intellect because of its agreement or disagreement with a present state?

Examine the following product of the *Imagination:* "The cataracts blow their trumpets from the steep." What is it but a blending founded upon the agreement of the emotions produced by the trumpets and falling waters?

Thus far in the discussion agreements have had prominence in reconciling the so-called faculties of the intellect to the theory of three attributes, and three alone. But is not the intellect engaged as well in each exercise with perception of differences? Is not discrimination the foundation of a perception of agreement? Can a resemblance be perceived except by the light of differences already perceived? And does not the intellect after each exercise retain what it has acquired, just as a plant retains the elements it has stored from the air and earth? Could the intellect abstract without retaining the objects to be compared? Would there be any thing to abstract unless they were thus held? Could the intellect judge without retaining the notion of the class as a basis with which to compare the new object? Could the intellect make the successive steps required to reach the act known as reason without holding over the fruitage of each effort to serve as the basis for the succeeding comparison?

An evident corollary of this theory is that a certain order must exist in the recurring occasions for the exercise of the three attributes. Reflection upon what has been said in respect to Reason will reveal clearly the order of progression to the assimilation of any principle.

Observing narrowly an intellect in its advance to assimilation of truth, three steps* are apparent, viz: (1) perceiving objects; (2) distinguishing resemblances and differences, and (3) discovering the truth which is a content of the resemblances. During this process the sense-objects have become thought-objects, and the intellect, retaining only those parts which are essential to the truth assimilated, perceives the objects more clearly than at first.

Assimilated *principles* are retained by the intellect as thought-objects, and these, as occasion arises for an exercise of the will by an individual, are, (1) perceived, (2) compared with reference to their fitness to the occasion, and some content of their relations (3) taken as a law for action.

That every man in every important act of his life does exercise his intellect in deciding as to his course in that case, before exercising his will, can be illustrated by an occurrence in every-day life: One sees a man leave his house prepared to go to his daily work, sees him pause, look round carefully, return, and shortly after reappear carrying an umbrella. What has passed in his mind? The sultry state of the atmosphere, the direction of the wind, the distinctness of sounds, the presence or absence of this or that, many things, in fact, which are retained by his intellect as thought-objects, by the sensations which their representatives in nature produce, have aroused his attention. His intellect at once instituted a comparison among them, extending its view to embrace others with which they were linked, concerning rain, its effects, the value of life, the worth of an umbrella as protection, etc. From this comprehensive group his intellect was able promptly

---

* The three acts of the intellect here pointed out will, for convenience, hereafter in the text be called (1) perceiving, (2) comparing, and (3) assimilating.

to make a law for his guidance. He probably foresaw it would be necessary for him to be exposed during the day, and he prepared himself.

Suppose, now, that after pausing and noting the appearance of things, he had gone on, how can we account for it? He has simply taken other links of the chain as his law. He remembers, perhaps, that he will not have to leave his office during the day, and sees that he can reach there before the rain. Or perhaps he recalls that he has another umbrella at his office for such contingencies.

To illustrate the relations of these intellect-acts, viz., Perceiving, Comparing, and Assimilating to mind growth, two simple examples are here given.

Suppose the task be to classify a number of marbles. (1) Perceiving takes place. (2) Comparing follows, which brings to view certain resemblances, as color, size, value, etc. (3) Selection of one, as "color," for the guiding principle, the classification is readily made. For the second illustration, suppose the task be to discover the principle upon which depends the form of axle-nuts of a buggy. (1) By perceiving, the student is able to distinguish the nuts and their parts, viz., threads, form, motion, orifices, etc., and also to distinguish the wheels and their parts to which the nuts are closely related. (2) By comparing, he perceives certain resemblances, viz., fastenings, covers for holding grease, *which extend throughout*. Persisting, he finds a resemblance in the direction of the threads in two of them. (3) With this principle the nuts are classified as left-handed and right-handed. Seeking to reconcile this difference to the resemblance "fastenings," he arrives at the principle.

The work of the teacher in these two illustrations (if we impose the condition of the learner having a teacher) would manifestly be to let the mind act alone and for itself in arriving at the principle. When he has supplied the material, his after-work should be simply to direct the learner in his investigation by proper questions. These modes of existence of the intellect correspond to the questions *what, how,* and *why,* and the teacher is in his proper sphere when he supplies the stimulus in each mode indicated by these interrogatories.

The remarkable parallelism in the three examples noted above, in that the action of the intellect in each is the same, leads to the conclusion that the acts resulting from the will taking the assimilated truth as its guide in each case are alike in kind, and are therefore phenomena of the same thing. If the acts of the man in the first illustration are phenomena of character—and who can deny that they are?—then, proceeding to classify the marbles in the second case, or doing any thing guided by the truth assimilated in the third illustration, are also phenomena of character.

And if this conclusion is true, then is it not clear that intellect-culture is the greatest factor in producing marked character both in individuals and in peoples?

Intellect development (on true principles) and character education are so related that they go forward together; or, in other words, that a weak or vicious character in a man [in the sense in which these terms are generally understood] results from deficient or misdirected intellectual training, and that a strong or a virtuous character is the direct effect of enlarged intellectual teaching that neglects no relation man sustains either to the Supreme, to his fellows, or to the world of organic and inorganic objects that constitutes his environment.

The only intellect to which one has full access is his own, and this discussion will be better understood if the reader make careful tests of what is claimed to be true by close observations on his own mental processes in learning.

Observation upon the workings of one's own mind discovers that it forms thought-objects which correspond to sense-objects, that thought-unities are created that represent groups or families of sense-objects, and that thought-verities (principles) are apprehended that represent the relations of sense-objects and groups of sense-objects.

Furthermore, the observer of his own mind will see that in the affairs of life he is constantly deciding as to his action in this or that by means of thought-verities acting as laws established by his reason for the government of his conduct.

Self-observation will convince a candid mind that the art of teaching intellect aright consists in conducting it *successfully* and *consciously* through the three processes, viz: Intellect-perceiving, intellect-comparing, and intellect-assimilating, and in the order named.*

If truth and not error is *assimilated*, then the teaching has been *successful;* if the learner knows that he is *assimilating* new truths day by day, then his teaching has been *conscious*. The pupil whose intellect has been *successfully* and *consciously* taught will consciously and successfully—so benign is the influence of truth—apply these same processes in the affairs of life; he will be able to *perceive* more clearly, *compare* more correctly, and to *assimilate* more advantageously than one who has been taught in a hap-hazard way, or who is self-taught. He will, in consequence, attain success more readily (having fewer things to learn anew) than his *confrères*, the self-taught and wrong-taught.

These processes utilized by the educated man become his character; the measure of character is power in utilization.

It follows, then, that the teacher who leads a pupil *successfully* and *consciously* along the pathway of his development adds intensity to his character.

Now if this is true, viz: that intellect-education and character-development are the same in *kind*, *i. e.*, that what develops (intensifies) the one develops the other, it follows that the problem of right moral training is solved if the true relations of like entities (man to man, brother to brother, citizen to

---

* It is not intended to assert that a period of life, say of years in duration, should be devoted to each. The truth is, that in a very short interval of time the intellect may act in each phase of its existence: it does so from the beginning. The "order named" is important, because the completed act, *i. e.*, assimilation, is the result of the other two. In the phenomena of character, which is largely the fruitage of intellectual effort, these same processes manifest themselves almost instantaneously.

citizen, etc., etc.) be made a part of the intellectual equipment of every pupil. This conclusion, which in effect puts the teacher in the attitude of being the greatest factor in the formation of moral character, brings up naturally the question of his responsibility. In determining this, other *data* enter into the problem; the natural bias of the child, the previous treatment he has had, and like considerations varying in each case. If the natural bent of a child is to the right, it is a good thing to make him strong in intellect and character by education; if, on the contrary, his natural bias is to the wrong, it would be better, *perhaps*, to leave him uneducated. It would certainly be better to leave him so if his evil tendencies are not destroyed or greatly modified by his course of training. But who is to judge? Clearly it is no man's province to say who shall or who shall not be educated. It follows, then, that society owes to each of its members a training adequate to make him self-sustaining; and in order that no natural thief shall be endowed with power to prey more successfully upon his fellows, the further duty is entailed of making general education moral as well as intellectual. This can be done only by putting into the curriculum those elements which are the foundation for correct principles.

The conclusions based upon self-observation thus far drawn will be apparent to any one who makes a careful study of his own intellect.

But are they true, and can they be confirmed by observations upon actual teaching? The argument following is based upon observations made in teaching, and can be verified by any one who has had sufficient experience as a teacher.

In the sphere of teacher one must assume that his pupil has an intellect like in kind to his own, but differing in degree, and proceed accordingly. He must treat it also as a complex whole. As is the body, so is the mind. One sees a man start from home to his place of business; his body moves, but at the same time his heart is beating, his blood is coursing, his feet are stepping, his hands are swinging, his muscles alternately tensing and relaxing, and his eyes are turning here and there. His whole physical being, in fact, is in action, each part contributing to make up the grand phenomenon called walking. A very simple thing is this, upon a cursory view, but a very complex thing when it is analyzed. Such is the mind the teacher undertakes to train, equally complex, and more difficult to analyze because its phenomena are intangible; and especially to teachers, because they are wont, in this, as in all things (such is the influence of our system of education), to take what some one says for the truth instead of striving each for himself, through observations on himself and his pupils, to assimilate the true laws of teaching.

To be the cause of a *healthful, positive* expression of the intellect in the consciousness of the learner, the teacher must be able to command the *attention* of that learner so as to cause him to know one thought-object from another, and to know numbers of them; he must be able, by directing the *memory*, to lead the learner to perceive the relations between his thought-objects, *i. e.*, their resemblances, their differences, and their capabilities for combination; he must also be able to inspire the *imagination* of the learner to work out combinations for himself; and lastly, he must be able to direct the *will* of the learner by making him cognizant of the fact that what new combinations he has made are a part of his mental structure, and are to be used for his own good. (What is for his good being what is good for society, of which he is but a part, the good of society itself at the same time being the all-wise *will* of the Infinite.) Truly, a healthful movement of the intellect is a complex and sublime spectacle! And verily, he who brings it about in "one of these little ones" hath his reward in the approving smile of the Father of All!

To summarize what has just been elaborated is to say: The mind is a complex whole, and must be treated as such if healthfully trained. The teacher fails in his aim if he fails to know that *attention, memory,* and *imagination* are but the tools by which the pupil does his work, and that intellect-culture and character are the completed products of that work. He fails also to healthfully educate if he fails to discern his true relations to his pupils. He can not give the pupil the tools, but he can and he must keep them sharpened; he can not build the structure, but he can and ought to draw the plan.

There is in no case a healthful action of the intellect of the learner unless the three modes of action defined and illustrated heretofore exist at the same time.*

When the human being through reflection begins to appropriate principles he has learned as laws for his guidance in the affairs of life, he is developing character. That character is intensified in the same degree as his power to apply his intellect in the discovery of truth is intensified. In other words, strength of character and intellectual power exist together. Teaching the intellect affects the character in *degree* in all cases. But it can be made to affect it in *kind* as well by a judicious selection of thought-objects for the pupil. And herein lies the responsibility of the teacher. He must, by a proper choice of material, exercise those emotions of his pupil that will cause him to make a wise choice in principles for his guidance. Now, if principles are selected (for the pupil to discover) that are inherent in relations of himself to his fellow pupils, they will in time become fixed as laws with him, and he will have been *educated morally.*

It is to be observed that the *will* of the pupil becomes a factor in such results; that it is a factor and an important one

---

*"Time" is not here used in the sense of moment or instant, for it may be a much longer period. Any one who has reflected after the discovery of a truth or principle will observe that his thought-objects appear with a new force, and the thought-unities resulting shine with a new luster. They are, in fact, the *data* of the complete intellectual assimilation. It may be remarked here that the difference between man and the lower animals consists in this, that they never abstract a principle out of their thought-unities, nor is it certain that they even perceive the thought-verities existing as relations of thought-objects; reflection shows that man does all this and does it as one act. And this is what is meant by the phrase "at the same time."

in the education of character. It is a factor because it influences the choice in principles discovered, and it is important because, unless the pupil is allowed unhampered to exercise it, his education is unhealthful. His will must be guided, not broken. But how is the will to be guided? Evidently by exercising the emotions that are healthful in tendency. But how is this to be done? One evident answer is, that it must be done systematically; this refers to the theory that should govern the practice.

But there is another answer that should shape the method to be used, and this answer is paramount. If this effort to improve the art of teaching succeeds in doing good, it will be because the great lesson it shall convey is, that the welfare of the pupil in after-life is dependent to a very great degree upon the *method* used in training him. Method, not methods, is the term used, and the fact can not be too much emphasized that the *one* method should control in all efforts of the teacher in ethics as well as in science.

Given the proper *data*, the manner of proceeding is easily determined. Now the proper *data* for correct moral development are found in the happenings of every-day life at school and at home, in the history of individuals, of neighborhoods, and of nations, and also in stories.

The theory and practice of schools in the sphere of moral training has inclined too much to story telling and story reading. This is erroneous, for the reason that a story is a work of art. The author is not a teacher, and has not the *sole* end in view of engrafting a true principle upon the moral nature of a responsible human being. His art requires certain climaxes to be wrought in as part of the woof of his story. Rewards and punishments are an invariable accompaniment to the happy ending of a story. For unless it *does* end well it will never go to press for a second edition. This utilitarian consideration largely shapes the form of stories.

But there is another and a graver objection to the sole use of this as a method. It is this: In stories the motives of the actors and their choice of courses of action are rarely brought out fully. For obvious reasons the full details of environment are never brought to the view of the reader-pupil, and hence his principles are only approximately true. The character resulting from a course of training through stories will always lack in force and independence, for the very apparent reason that the pupil in acquiring it was a passive imitator. He is a fit subject, when turned free, for the wiles of the political demagogue, inasmuch as he has never thought for himself in *assimilating* principles.

The objection to making history alone the basis of moral training is, that it is barren of material for all grades of schools. The great lessons of policy in governmental affairs and in affairs of like magnitude are of such gravity that they do not command the attention of young pupils. They are of great value in high-school work, and their use with such pupils as are just ready to struggle with the problems of citizenship can not be too highly commended. But things nearer home, things within the world of the little ones, are needed for primary schools.

Hypothetical cases, and cases of real happening where the names of the parties concerned can be withheld, are the best possible material for this work. A good story made hypothetical may be used for moral lessons. It is important that the instruction in every case, whatever the material, should be hypothetical, as by this means only can all the *thought-objects* and *thought-unities*, which constitute the whole environment of the *thought-verity* (principle) it is designed to cause the pupil at that particular lesson to *assimilate*, be brought together.

As to conduct of lesson: Principles, as they shape themselves in the minds of pupils, ought to be announced by those who conceive them. These ought to be taken up and discussed by the teacher and pupils. If erroneous, the missing *data* which will make them true can be supplied by any one who has discovered them.

Moral lessons conducted in this way, after the hypothetical method, universal in scientific investigation, give exercise to the will and leave it free to act.

This latter consideration is of great importance, because no fact is clearer than that the will must be left unfettered in order to the development of a character that will do right for the right's sake. We all applaud the immortal sentiment expressed by Clay in the utterance, "I would rather be *right* than President," and we despise any other groundwork as the motive for our actions. The teacher should prayerfully lead his pupils to reach this noble ideal.

POSTULATES.

In the formulated expression of the postulates and explanations attached, presented in this section, the word "whole" is used to name all the thought-objects contributing to any complete intellectual action. These *thought-objec's* through their relations disclose a truth; they are in this sense a separate group; they are spoken of as a "whole."

Where "repetition" is enjoined in the explanations it is meant not to use the same sense-objects or whatever else constitutes the "whole" for that lesson, but others for each repetition. Many repetitions are sometimes necessary to enable all members of a class to grasp a truth.

I. It is only through a "whole" as a medium that the intellect assimilates any truth.

This postulate assumes that the work of the teacher involves (1) a comprehension of the truth it is his intention to impress at any given lesson; (2) a knowledge of all the elements (thought-objects) whose relations hold this truth as a content, and (3) the bringing of these elements within the mental view of the pupil.

After placing the *data*, which must be a "whole," before the pupil, questioning in the domain of "what" will lead him to *perceive* all the elements. Questioning in the domain of "how," which includes "when" and "where," will cause him to see *differences* and *agreements*. The question "why" will lead to the discovery of the truth, which is the objective point of the lesson. For practical illustrations of the application of this postulate see pages 26 and 47.

II. Assimilation of truth is a self-act, and is on occasion.

This postulate assumes that the learning of every truth is accidental to the intellect assimilating it. Let the conditions exist of an intellect sufficiently developed to receive it and a "whole" comprehensive enough to contain it, and the truth is born upon their conjunction. The teacher is only one of the circumstances that combine to bring the proper conditions into existence.

This postulate accounts for the fact, often mentioned as singular, that many of our greatest inventions were the results of accidental combinations.

As inferences from it may be mentioned the following: The will of the learner does not cause him to learn; neither can the will of the teacher operate to cause assimilation of truth; excessive exertions of the will by either toward this end tend to defeat it; the will of the pupil should be exercised in giving attention, the will of the teacher in building, repairing, and enlarging the "whole," or in exchanging it for another.

III. Formulating truth (language) follows the assimilation of it.

IV. Language is necessary, and must become generic in order to any great intellectual development.

These two postulates are important, inasmuch as there are many mistakes made by teachers growing out of ignorance or disregard of what is assumed in them. It seems to be true that the mind is content to hold a truth without language so long as it sees it in the relations of one group or "whole." But as soon as it perceives the same truth in another group a demand is born for symbols, as associations, by which to retain the enlarged view now given to it. This demand and its application are illustrated by lessons on pages 27 and 41. That repetition is necessary in teaching is an inference from these postulates. It is necessary (1) in order to create the demand for symbols, thereby securing their retention with the proper meanings, and (2) to fix them in the memory with their generic meanings.

V. The intellect is primarily analytical, and secondarily synthetical in tendency.

The intellect of a learner looks out upon nature or upon a "whole" contrived by his teacher, and all at first glance is chaos. Soon his intellect-perceiving enables him to separate the various objects in view. These objects in nature or in the artificial grouping are themselves units. If the attention is fixed upon one of them, the intellect separates it into its parts, and so on for the others. This process is analysis, and is the primary act of intellect. Transferring the attention from one to the many brings resemblances and differences to consciousness. These relations hold truths as contents which are seized by the intellect. Operating under conceived principles, the intellect proceeds to make new units which it did not apprehend at first glance. This grouping act of the intellect, which seems historically to follow analysis, is synthesis. It begins with the first seizure of a principle; it is that factor which distinguishes the mind of man from that of a lower animal; it is the parent of language.

With this postulate governing him, a teacher can so question his pupil as to lead him far enough in analysis to prepare him for certain success on the other road. When synthesis has accomplished its purpose of making a new "whole" for subsequent analysis, the teacher's work is done for that stage of development.

In any science principles taught are necessarily related to each other, and at every stage it will be necessary for the teacher to group facts that have been learned as species out of which the intellect of the learner shall be made to construct new generalizations. This fact, that truths learned are species of higher genera of truths, makes it apparent that the human intellect is capable of endless development. The other fact noted, that the principles of a science are related, not detached, suggests with a force not to be questioned that there is a law of identity in every science which contains all others.

VI. All intellectual processes are at first unconscious.

This postulate requires the most delicate management on the part of the teacher, in order to prevent doing irreparable injury to those pupils who need encouragement in their efforts. The period of unconsciousness after the discovery of a truth varies in different individuals, and herein lies the danger. The teacher should exercise the greatest care in observing, to prevent mistakes in judgment, which will lead him to censure where it is not deserved.

VII. Intellects differ in degree, not in kind.

This postulate demands the same groupings of "wholes" for all grades of intellect. Since repetition is enjoined by postulates III and IV, as essential to successful teaching, the opportunity is here afforded the teacher to so adapt his exercises as to tax the various grades of intellect in the class each to its limit, by making the first "whole" probable to the highest grade only. The lower grades will not be injured, but be helped by their efforts to assimilate through a "whole" not adapted to them. A subsequent effort will more surely succeed after the same truth has been assimilated through an easier "whole."

VIII. The mind, having assimilated a truth by intellectual action, has an innate tendency to apply it.

This postulate announces a fact which is important to the teacher, inasmuch as it indicates that he is largely responsible for the moral training of his pupil. Its phenomena are seen chiefly in the development of character.

Now, how can the teacher bring about the recall by the pupil of the principle or law that should govern his will in any case with such authority as will give it domination?

1. The pupil must assimilate it under such circumstances originally as are parallel to finding a treasure in a hollow tree: no hint of its existence must be given him.

2. The teacher must invest the finding with a multiplicity of *associations*, in order to provide for its recall in any contingency in which it may be needed by the individual.

Take the principle, "Thou shalt not steal," for example. Suppose a pupil's teaching only covers cases of taking money, clothing, watermelons, etc., when he could get along without them, or the owner could well spare them. Suppose, now, that individual to be starving or naked, or to have a hungry family dependent on him, and an opportunity is offered to steal, would he have a principle that would dominate his will? Assuredly not. Can we not account for those cases of embezzlement and official stealing, now so common, by there having been some *hypotheses* left out of the "whole," through which the embezzler assimilated his "Thou shalt not steal."

A curriculum of moral lessons might be contrived, taking such abstractions as *honesty, friendship, politeness, candor, charity, kindness*, etc., etc., as its basis. To teach any word so that it will go into the vocabulary is to follow Postulate IV. Now, when these words have been made *generic* by teaching, has the pupil not also [possibly] been caused to assimilate a law that will tend to dominate his will when necessary?

PRACTICAL LESSONS.

The three primary attributes of the Intellect, viz., a *Consciousness of Differences*, a *Consciousness of Agreement*, and *Conscious or Unconscious Retentiveness*, must ever be kept in memory by the teacher in reading this section. And he must also bear in mind the fact that the products of mind action resulting from these are: (1) *Thought-objects;* (2) *Relations of Thought-objects*, founded on Agreements and Differences; and (3) *Truths*, as contents of these relations. And a third fact, without which all teaching would be purposeless, must ever guide him, viz: A *Truth* once existent, the mind by a natural bias tends to apply it, and thus becomes self-active.

The eight postulates given, while originally discovered and formulated from observations made on experiments and tests with classes, will be found to give full and logical expression to the facts of mind noticed above.

It is not desirable to separate this work into lessons, for it is not to be imitated. The intention is to give more forcible expression to what has been already said, and to make clear that the theory of this Monograph admits of easy practice. Yet, if any one attempts from one reading alone to apply these postulates, he will almost surely fail. It will require much study, much reflection, and repeated trials to succeed. It is the very simplicity of the whole thing that will puzzle the one who tries it.

The reader will find the word "repetition" often used. Let it be understood that this system forbids sameness in repetition; the same objects are in the kaleidoscope, but as it is turned slowly around there is endless variety of beautiful colors and symmetrical forms. Repetition refers alone to the truth or principle; Nature's resources for the expression of the same principle are apparently infinite; the teacher must, in teaching principles, become as Nature is, the parent of variety. The *particular* method must change with the number, the advancement and the character of the pupils, and with the subject-matter. The *esprit de corps* also has much to do with deciding details.

Illustrations are given in Arithmetic, Language, Geography, Ethics, Algebra, and Geometry; but it is believed that a like application of the Theory may be made in any and every science.

ARITHMETIC.

Nearly all the principles of arithmetic are embraced in this outline. Each is a species of some following one, and a genus of some one that precedes it. It is not pretended that this series of principles is the only method for arithmetic. Other species and genera may be used. This is the best so far discovered. Each principle is to be taught with distinct "wholes." [See Post. I.] With primary pupils the objects at first used should be blocks, or similar things, which in manipulation remain separated to the eye. Later, objects like straws, which in part lose their identity in handling, and still later, cards or sheets of paper, which in a greater degree are obscured, should be used. Finally, objects, as cups of water, which entirely disappear as separate units, ought to be used.

In all the work the pupil must be led to discover the principle, the teacher guiding by proper questions. In formulating the principle for future use the teacher must perfect the crude expression given to it by the pupil. It is not important to have the exact language used in this presentation of principles.

When the figures are the objects used, as in Prin. 8^I, no other objects can be used.

PRINCIPLES.

(1) Totals or Wholes are the same when all their parts are the same.

(2) A whole is all its parts put together.

(3) A whole is increased by the increase of any part.

(4) A whole is decreased by the decrease of any part.

(5) A whole is multiplied by multiplying every part.

(6) A whole is divided by dividing every part.

(7) When all the parts of any whole are of the same size or equal, the part is a unit, and the number of equal parts is a coefficient, and the total is a named-whole, or a measured quantity.

(8) A named-whole is multiplied either by multiplying the coefficient or unit.

(9) A named-whole is divided either by dividing the coefficient or unit.

(10) Interchanging the coefficient and the number of things in the unit gives same named-whole.

In other relations, by change of names, the coefficient becomes the multiplier, the unit becomes the multiplicand, and the named-whole becomes the product, and the 8th and 9th principles become:

$(8)^1$ Multiply either the multiplier or multiplicand and the product is multiplied.

$(9)^1$ Divide either the multiplier or multiplicand and the product is divided.

Omitting the objects, the multiplier and multiplicand become factors, and principles $(8)^1$ and $(9)^1$ become:

$(8)^1_1$ To multiply either of two factors multiplies their product.

$(9)^1_1$ To divide either of two factors divides their product.

Applying 10th principle to $(8)^1_1$ and $(9)^1_1$, and repeating the application, gives:

$(10)^1$ Any order of the same factors gives the same product.

(10)^{II} The prime factors of the product of any number of composite factors are all the prime factors of the composite numbers put together.

(10)^{III} The factors of the H. C. D. are all the common factors.

(10)^{IV} The factors of the L. C. M. are all the factors, common and not common.

(8)$^{II}_{I}$ To multiply *any* factor multiplies the product.

(9)$^{II}_{I}$ To divide *any* factor divides the product.

(11) The how much larger or smaller two quantities taken separately are than a third quantity, determines the how much larger or smaller one quantity is than the other.

(12) The subtraction of one quantity from another, and of the remainder from the smaller, repeating till nothing remains, the last subtrahend used is the highest unit common to both.

If the condition be imposed that a variable product of two factors shall have one factor constant, (8)$^{II}_{I}$ and (9)$^{II}_{I}$ give:

(13) The direct proportion.

If the condition be imposed that a product of two factors be constant, (8)$^{II}_{I}$ and (9)$^{II}_{I}$ give:

(14) The indirect proportion.

If conditions be imposed that a given number of things of one kind are to be put together in a whole every time a given number of things of another kind are put together in a whole, then to find a new whole of the latter kind for a given whole of the former kind, gives:

(15) If $a = \supset = b$
   then $a^1 = \supset = (a^1 \div a) \times b$ or,

(16) If $a = \supset = b$
   then $a^1 = \supset = (b \div a) \times b^1$.

Suggestions follow as to practice in teaching these principles.

Prin. 1. Except this principle be thoroughly assimilated by the pupil, failure in all the others is quite sure. Take a number of objects (blocks or straws, etc.), without counting, and ask the pupil to make a pile with as many in it, also without counting. Repeat the process a number of times. If the pupil can write, let him try to write on his pad or slate what he has been doing; * if he can not write, let him state what he has done. When he thoroughly apprehends *what* he has done, then ask him how the piles are alike. When he has discovered that they are alike in kind and number, then ask him to state *how* he knows they are alike in number and kind. When he can answer this question, then ask him to write down, with figures, the name of the first pile. To this end he must count it. When he has written the name of the first pile, ask him to write the name of the second pile. He will start to count that pile also. This must be prevented. Let him read over what he has discovered as to the respects in which the piles are alike. When he has written down the second pile, then put on the blackboard the results thus:

8 blocks   8 blocks.

Now ask him to write between the names in what respects they are alike. When he has written, 8 blocks are in number and kind like 8 blocks, then inform him that a sign is used to express the same thing, and put on the board 8 blocks = 8 blocks, and ask the pupil to write what the sign = means. When he is able to write, = means that 8 blocks are in kind and number like 8 blocks, he has made an important step. Repetition of the whole process must follow until he writes, = means alike in number and kind. Then take any two objects of the same kind, as two chairs, and enter into details of resemblances. Weigh one chair, or estimate its weight, and ask for the weight of the other. Take two books of the same edition, open at any page, and ask pupil to read what is in the other book at same place, handing him the open book. Do not be surprised if he wants the other book! Time sufficient should be given to secure a perfect assimilation of this principle.

<small>* The pupil must be required to do this throughout the course.</small>

(2) Let the pupil make two wholes, the same in number and kind as before. Ask him to separate one pile into two parts, different in size. Ask him in what respects the one pile is like the two piles. When he states, "Same in number and kind," ask for differences. When he states, "One is in two parts, and in the other all are in one pile," then ask him to write down the piles, one after the other. Let him count every pile. Then give him two piles with different numbers in them, and ask him to make one pile as large as both without counting. When he has done this, ask questions as before, and let him write down the names of piles as before. On the board write results thus:

5 blocks 3 blocks 8 blocks.

Ask the pupil to put in signs to give relations. If he can not use the signs, then so conduct the exercises as to induce him to write, "5 blocks put into one pile with 3 blocks are the same in number and kind as 8 blocks," or something equivalent, and then give the signs, thus:

5 blocks + 3 blocks = 8 blocks.

Repeat, by giving the pupil three unequal piles, and ask him to make one pile as large as the three without counting, and go through all the steps to

7 blocks + 3 blocks + 2 blocks = 12 blocks.

Continue in repetition, increasing the number of parts.

(3) Give the pupil three unequal piles, and ask him to make one pile as large as the three without counting. Then form three other piles, each as large as the former, and with a whole for them, all without counting. Repeat until he has as many sets of piles as there are piles in one set. Then let the pupil form three equal piles without counting. Now ask him to put one of these latter piles with the first pile of the first set. Ask him if the large pile is a whole for the three piles. He will answer, "No." Ask him to make it a whole for them, and he will immediately put one of the equal piles

with the whole. Repeat this process with second and third sets, the only change being to put one of the extra equal piles with the second of the three piles; do likewise with third set. Repeat until the pupil is familiar with the process, and can write it up. Then, as the steps are made with objects, let each be written up with figures on pads or slates, and then follow on the board, thus:

5 blocks + 3 blocks + 4 blocks = 12 blocks.
6 blocks   = 6 blocks.
―――――――――――――――――――――――――――――――――――
11 blocks + 3 blocks + 4 blocks = 18 blocks.

5 blocks + 3 blocks + 4 blocks = 12 blocks.
           6 blocks   = 6 blocks.
―――――――――――――――――――――――――――――――――――
5 blocks + 9 blocks + 4 blocks = 18 blocks.

5 blocks + 3 blocks + 4 blocks = 12 blocks.
                      6 blocks = 6 blocks.
―――――――――――――――――――――――――――――――――――
5 blocks + 3 blocks + 10 blocks = 18 blocks.

Ask for and secure resemblances and differences of the three processes as they appear on the board.

(4) Is to be taught in a precisely similar manner to the 3d principle.

(5) Give the pupil two unequal piles, and ask him to make one pile as large as both. Then ask him to make new piles, putting two straws in the new piles for every one straw in the *parts;* then to make a whole for his new parts. Then let him compare the number in the new whole to the number in the old whole. He will answer, "Two for one." Ask him how he knows that the new whole has two straws for every one straw in the old whole, when he did not make the new whole in that way. If he can not answer, repeat until he can see the reason for the fact. Then, in repeating, let him make two piles the same size as each part of old whole, and put these equal piles together—another way to put two for one. Gradually introduce the expressions, "two piles for

one pile," and "two times one pile," so that the pupil understands that "two straws for one straw," gives same results as "two piles for one pile," and understands the force of the expression "*two times.*" When pupils are prepared for it, let figures be used, thus:

4 sts. + 3 sts. = 7 sts.   Two for one gives
8 sts. + 6 sts. = 14 sts., all of which is to be written from actual work with things. Then put, thus:

$$\frac{4 \text{ sts.} + 3 \text{ sts.} = 7 \text{ sts.}}{8 \text{ sts.} + 6 \text{ sts.} = 14 \text{ sts.}} \quad 2 = 2$$

In repetition vary the number of parts, and the number *for* one, until the pupil is perfectly familiar with the steps. Like the (1) principle, this principle requires much time and patience.

(6) To be taught precisely as principle (5), except to take one straw in the new parts for every two straws in the old parts, etc.

(7) Give the pupil, say, twelve straws, and ask him to give each of three pupils an equal share without counting. Give the pupil any number of straws, and ask him to separate them into a given number of equal parts. When the pupil can do this readily, then let him form equal wholes, and ask him to separate one of the wholes into, say, three equal parts. Ask questions *what, how,* and *why,* as before. Ask him to write up in figures. He writes, 4 sts. + 4 sts. + 4 sts. = 12 sts. Give him three books, and ask him to write that up. He will write, 3 books. Ask him to write up same number of any objects. He writes, 3 pencils, 3 slates, etc. Now ask him to do the same with the piles of straw, and perhaps he will write, 3 piles of straw. Ask for name of pile. He answers, 4 sts. Now he will probably write, 3 4 sts. Direct him to use the comma, thus: 3, 4 sts. Repeat until the pupil is familiar with the naming.

Review principles (3), (4), (5), and (6) at this point, using two or more straws in lieu of one as a counter.

(8) Is taught precisely as the 5th principle, with perfectly apparent changes.

(9) To be taught as (8) or as (6).

(10) Give the pupil 12 straws, and ask him to make, without counting, another whole of the same size. Then ask him to separate one of the wholes into three equal parts. Then ask him to form new parts, by taking one straw from each of the three parts until all are gone. Then ask him to make a new whole for the new four equal parts. Ask for relation of this new whole to the old whole. When he answers that they are the same in number and kind, ask how he knows that fact. Repeat this process with different numbers of equal piles until the pupil assimilates this principle, which is so very important to much that follows.

How $(8)^I$, $(9)^I$, $(8)^I_I$, $(9)^I_I$, etc., grow out of the other principles from which they derive their name, must be apparent, on reflection, and to teach them is but a repetition of the original principle with slight changes.

(11) Make three equal piles of straws before the whole class without counting them. Call them respectively A, B, and C. Add two straws to pile A and five straws to pile C, and ask the class to compare the number in A to the number in C. Make all possible variations with the same numbers in A and C, but let B remain the same. Let the pupils write up as follows:

   A has 3 straws more than B.
   C has 5 straws more than B.
   $\therefore$ A has 2 straws less than C.
   A has 3 straws less than B.
   C has 5 straws less than B.
   $\therefore$ A has 2 straws more than C, etc., etc.

It is well here to show, at this point, the algebraic signs applicable:

$+ 3 - (+ 5) = -2$, first example above.
$- 3 - (- 5) = +2$, second example above.*

---

* NOTE—This illustration gives eight cases.

The average pupil does this work without much trouble.

(12) Is taught by taking any two piles of straws with different numbers and going through the process indicated.

(13) By the use of numbers the following generic statement is easily taught. Let A be the variable product and B the variable factor and C the constant factor; then multiplying or dividing B multiplies or divides A, whence $A \div A^1 = B \div B^1$, whence $A : A^1 = B : B^1$, the direct proportion.

$$A = B \cdot C$$
$$A^1 = B^1 \cdot C$$

(14) By the use of numbers the following is likewise easily taught. Let A be the constant product and B and C the variable factors; then, multiplying B divides C, whence $B \div B^1 = C^1 \div C$, or $B : B^1 = C^1 : C$, the indirect proportion.

$$A = B \cdot C$$
$$A = B^1 \cdot C^1$$

(15) (16) Are so easily taught by the use of straws and blocks that illustration is not needed.

HOW TO USE EXAMPLES FROM TEXT-BOOKS.

Alternating with and supplementing the work already given, much practice by the pupil must be had in working problems. These may be originated by the teacher, or taken from books. In every case they should be made to serve as additional " wholes " to secure assimilation of principles.

It is thought to be necessary here, before leaving the subject, to enter into details somewhat as to how to use the examples so as to secure the end desired, *i. e.*, to make them repetitions. It is to be noted that examples from books have not been recommended till after the principle has been assimilated through objective teaching. This recommendation, therefore, presumes the existence of the principle in the mind of the pupil, although in an inchoate state. The first question when an example is presented should be, " What principle is contained here?" A failure to get the proper answer need not discourage the teacher, as it is for some time the rule and not the exception.

Questioning in the domain of "what," "how," and "why," will lead to its discovery and to the proper solution. With large classes it is well to have all do simultaneously on pads or slates what the teacher does on the board in response to answers to his questions.

In general, a number of problems can be treated in a lesson. After this study of a lesson, the whole work should be erased, and the pupils required to make an *exact* reproduction of it for the next time. This reproduction lesson is a valuable one, as it leads the way to independent work by steps possible of accomplishment by all.

More difficult practice is secured by leaving all numbers blank in the example under consideration, proceeding by questions as before. Examples treated in this way may be left on pads, the requirement for the reproduction lesson being to fill the blanks, and bring solutions according to usual forms of written answers.

When the details of operations (addition, multiplication, etc.,) have become automatic through practice, and mistakes are no longer made, it is advisable to have solutions formulated by signs, to express the operations necessary.

NOTE—If a teacher instructs after this method throughout the whole course in numbers, the tables will be learned incidentally, just as the letters are learned through the application of the word method in teaching reading.

LANGUAGE.

The illustrations in language-work to follow will be embraced under the following headings: *Word Teaching, Reading,* and *Grammar.*

Introductory remarks are inserted here to elucidate the relations of the postulates to such work.

The necessity for language is felt by an individual who wishes to impart his thoughts to others or to himself; its convenience is felt by one who wishes to recall a principle in order to apply it, or a thought-object in order to compare it with others. It is pertinent to remark here that memorized definitions fail to serve the convenience of the learner. His own formulations only are available to him for progress in intellectual work. Constant opportunities ought, therefore, to be given him to write his own definitions, rules, or other principles assimilated.

What was said in regard to the necessity of language is of such importance to progress in its *use* that it is almost worthy of being formulated as a separate postulate. Its bearing upon teaching will be apparent when one reflects that unless the pupil has the motive to *impart* his knowledge at the time he gets it, then no *necessity* can exist for its use, and he will lapse into inattention during the lesson, or forget the fact afterward.

If the pupil is made conscious of what he learns [see page 10] the desired end will be reached, for he has the *giving* motive as an inheritance.

Thought-objects record themselves in language as *words, phrases, clauses,* and *sentences;* thought-unities take form as generic *words* and *sentences,* and thought-verities as *sentences,* either elliptical or complete.

When a tangible object has been *perceived,* and its associations with the individual perceiving are intimate, a necessity exists for a name for it. Proper names, as *Fido* and *William,* are the only formulations from intellect-perceiving.

When the second step, *comparing,* has been made by the intellect, class names, as, *horse, running, swiftly, black,* etc., are learned. Phrases expressive of relations, as, *with a stick, on a fence, in a field,* are also conceived. Complex relations, as, *The black horse runs in a field, The tree is bending before the wind,* are likewise apprehended at this stage.

When the intellect has completely acted in any case, a general truth or a universal truth has been assimilated. It exists as a content of certain relations of certain thought-objects that have been brought together as a "whole." Examples of such mind-action formulated are, *The wind has force, Sustenance is necessary to life.*

This analysis of the functions of language is thought to be necessary for the teacher to enable him to intelligently direct those under his charge. The following principles are recommended to teachers, to be used in the manner outlined below, in connection with both reading and grammar lessons. They will serve the purpose of "waking up" the pupil to a comprehension of what he does in talking, writing, reading, and hearing. Frequent repetitions are necessary to insure assimilation.

I. **Sentences are identical when all their words are identical.**
II. **Sentences vary in meaning as their words vary.**
III. **A sentence has essential parts which, put together, make up the meaning.**
IV. **Each modifier of the predicate decreases its horizon of meaning.** [The subject is regarded as a modifier.]

The following method of presenting the *data* for these principles, it is believed, will recommend itself for its simplicity and directness.

PRINCIPLE I.

Write two or three sentences exactly identical as far as the words that compose them are concerned, as:

Mary loves her doll.
Mary loves her doll.
Mary loves her doll.

Ask the following questions :*
Are these expressions alike in meaning?
There are very few who will not unreservedly answer, "Yes," to this question. If "yes" is the general answer, continue questioning in "what" after this manner, "How many parts (words) in each?" "What does Mary mean?"

---

* It is better to have answers written, as such a course secures effort on the part of each pupil.

"loves?" "her?" "doll?" Does Mary mean the same in each sentence? Division in opinion inevitably results at this point if the teacher has held the attention well.

Continue by questioning with "how." For example:

How do you know the Mary is the *same* in each sentence? Is there only one Mary in the world? All will agree that if different Marys are meant different meanings attach to the sentences.

Question further: "If the Marys are different, can the dolls be the same?" Agreement will again result in saying that the dolls are different. The class that is thus led to agree will also agree in saying that "Sentences are identical when their words or parts are the same in meaning," if the question is asked. A complete assimilation can be secured by announcing that the sentences *are* indentical in meaning, and then asking "why?"

PRINCIPLE II.

Make changes as follows:

1. *Mary loves her doll.*
2. *Mary loves her cat.*
3. *Mary loves her mother.*
4. *Mary loves her breakfast.*

Call for resemblances and differences in the separate units (sentences). Question in the domain of "what" until all the meanings in "loves" are brought to view according to its modifiers, *doll, cat, mother, breakfast*. There are also different meanings to "her" in the separate sentences which might be brought to view by questioning, but it will not be necessary to be exhaustive in analyzing the units into their parts. Compare (1) and (2) by questioning as to *how* the separate meanings result. If necessary, change "cat" to "doll" in (2), in order to make them identical. Compare others in the same way, keeping the intellect busy in observing "how" differences result.

Add other sentences to the group, such as:

5. *Mary loves my doll.*
6. *Mary loves everybody.*
7. *Mary loves a hot breakfast.*

Make the comparison of the new sentence with another in the group from which it differs in only one word, and the answer to "how" will take the form: By *changing* the "her" in (1) to "my" in (5). By changing "her mother" in (3) to "everybody" in (6), etc., etc. When the class have *perceived* and *compared* consciously in answer to "what" and "how," they will readily *assimilate* the principle in answer to the question, "Why do sentences vary in meaning?"

PRINCIPLE III.

Arrange the words of a short story in columns, thus:

air	the	Henry
John	threw	a
large	other	in
it	caught	ball
persons	into	William
every	and	his
hands	play	saw
enjoyed	them	several
their	one	at
much	very	it

Tell the class that these are the words of a story. Ask them to look over the list and tell what things happened. The result will no doubt be, *seeing, throwing, catching, playing, enjoying.*

Ask who did these things, and get, *William, John, Henry, persons.*

Ask when these things happened; the past form of the verbs will give a cue in this case.

Ask in what order the *happenings* took place. This will

result in getting *throwing, catching, seeing, and enjoying,* as the natural order of events.

After arranging who did the *throwing,* etc., the class are prepared to write the story, as follows:

"William threw a large ball into the air. Henry caught it in his hands. John and several other persons saw them at play. Every one enjoyed it very much."

On the first trial many of the minor modifiers will be overlooked. They can be supplied by asking questions like the following: What is *large* used for? *Into* what, do you suppose? *At* what? *Enjoyed* what? etc., etc.

When the complete story has been constructed, question upon the office of the several words used. This is but going over the same ground again, and it will be found that the pupils will answer promptly, as follows:

To tell what happened, to tell who did something, to tell where it was thrown, etc.

Lead them then to observe that each sentence has (1) a word *to tell what is said,* (2) a word *to tell what it is said of,* and (3) phrases or words to tell *kind, time, manner, place,* etc.

Call these *predicate, subject,* and *modifiers,* and have them point them out in other sentences. Several repetitions of this work, or something similar, will be necessary to secure complete assimilation of the principle.

PRINCIPLE IV.

Commence with part of a phrase, thus:

Into the,

and have the members of the class to suggest endings, as follows:

1. Into the { air / water / room / house / etc.

Combine into the generic phrase, *into something* or *somewhere*. Selecting one of the species, continue thus:

2. Into the air the
$$\begin{cases} \text{arrow} \\ \text{ball} \\ \text{bird} \\ \text{stone} \\ \text{etc.} \end{cases}$$

Proceeding as before, construct:

3. Into the air the arrow
$$\begin{cases} \text{sped} \\ \text{flew} \\ \text{shot} \\ \text{went} \\ \text{etc.} \end{cases}$$

Selecting again, complete the sentence:

4. Into the air the arrow sped.

Compare (1), (2), (3), and (4), with a view of making the assimilation that *sped* fixes the meaning of the whole.

Taking *sped* as the basis, construct the equivalent generalization:

Something somewhere sped.

Construct a horizon to represent this meaning, and smaller ones within it to represent the restricted meaning as modifiers are added, thus:

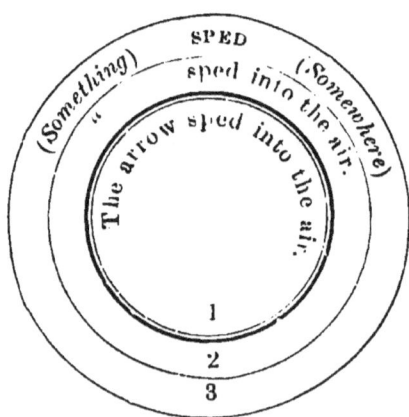

Numbering the horizons as in the diagram, and setting up a comparison among them, the pupil may be led to make the assimilation formulated by the principle.

Many repetitions, however, will be necessary in order to secure thorough mastery of it.

NOTE.—A complete generic idea involving every element may be expressed by the following formula:

Something, somewhere, sometime, somehow, somewhy, $\begin{cases} exists. \\ acts. \end{cases}$

The predicate or verb in assuming tense form expresses always *existence*, or its alternative *action*, and *generic time*, and holds elliptically the other elements of the idea. All modifiers of the predicate are but expressions of the character of certain elements in the idea seeking expression. If any particular element only demands a generic expression it does not assume form; if it exists in a specific degree some adjunct or word as a modifier of the elliptical form expresses it.

The modality of the idea is expressed by the particular form its language representative takes, viz., as a *statement*, as an *interrogatory*, or as a *command*.

The quantity of the idea is expressed by the modifiers as a group or whole. Illustrations are given below.

I. 1. *Something:* A night of storm.
   2. *Somewhere:* (held generically.)
   3. *Sometime:* (expressed in *followed*.)
   4. *Somehow:* (expressed in *followed*.)
   5. *Somewhy:* (held generically.)
   6. $\begin{cases} Exists: \\ Acts: \end{cases}$ followed a day of sunshine.
   7. Its *modality* is apparent in the fact that it is a statement.
   8. Compare:

A night of storm *follows* a day of sunshine,

Nights of storm $\begin{cases} were \\ are \end{cases}$ followed by $\begin{cases} a\ day \\ days \end{cases}$ of sunshine, or other expressions of similar ideas to that under analysis, and the *quantity* becomes apparent.

II. 1. *Something:* my father.
    6. *Exists; sometime:* lived.
    2. *Somewhere:* beside the Tyne.

The other constructive elements are held generically in "lived," and are therefore elliptical. The *modality* and *quantity* will be apparent through comparison.

III. 6. *Acts:* $\Big\}$ dawn and lend (thine aid).
    3. *Sometime:*
    4. *Somehow:* $\begin{cases} \text{on our darkness (modifies generic idea in "dawn").} \\ \text{us — (to us) (modifies generic idea in "lend").} \end{cases}$

"Thine aid" is a modifier of the elliptical object inhering in "lend." The other constructive elements are held generically in the predicate, and *modality* and *quantity* are apparent in the form.

Other examples are not necessary to make apparent the fact that every English sentence, whatever its mode, may be analyzed as the examples are by *comparing* with the generic sentence.

Reflection will show that if sentences are studied as "wholes" in this way, and comparisons made in the manner indicated, that the *assimilations* made by the pupils will be of the highest value to them in understanding what they read, and in expressing their thoughts with clearness and force.

WORD TEACHING.

When a child first enters school he has a large stock of words in his speaking vocabulary. The aim of the teacher should be, at this stage of his education, to make him acquainted with these in their written and printed forms.

This is the primary course of study in reading. By necessity some new words will be added to his vocabulary during the two or three years necessary to bring him up with what he already knows.

If this is well done, his after work in reading is easy. But at every stage of his education his teacher ought to present thoroughly all the new word material he encounters in his text-books.

An illustration is given below of how this should be done, both with words already in the vocabulary and with words it is desired to put there.

In this work the teacher should have Postulates III and IV in mind. The illustrations are taken from actual practice, the first with a class during their second month in school, the second with children entering upon their third year.

Teacher (writing the word "run" on a card): Who can tell me what that says?

Pupil (selected from a number who volunteered): It says *run*.

T.: Can *you* run?

The pupil assented, and after a little persuasion ran to his seat. The teacher then, to test their knowledge of the word, asked questions and got the following statements:

A boy can run.

A horse can run.

Inquiring as to the difference in the running, he found they associated it with the legs. This indicated that the meaning was not *generic* to them. The next question was, "Can a box run?" This produced a general laugh, and many emphatic "noes." "*Why* not?" asked the teacher of one pupil, who evidently had a reason in his mind. "Because it has no legs," was the prompt reply.

"Can a wagon run?" asked the teacher. There was some hesitation, but many answered, "Yes." "But it has no legs; how is that?" There was quiet for some time. At length a hand went up, and the very wise reply, "Its *wheels* are its legs," was modestly given. The teacher then illustrated the meaning of the word by calling attention to the clock which was *running* and to water on a sheet of paper, and left the word for another.

The *perceiving* powers of the children had been exercised in recognizing the different actions; their *comparing* powers had been exercised in observing the differences and resemblances in the actions. Their *assimilating* powers were probably exercised in getting a more generic meaning for the word. This latter was the aim of the teacher; how well he succeeded could only be known by testing the class at some subsequent lesson.

The next illustration is of a new word. A girl had asked to have the word "fatigued" from the reading lesson explained. The teacher persuaded her to run to and fro in the room a number of times. After she had done this she was asked how she felt. "I feel *tired*," was the reply. "*Some* people would say *fatigued*," remarked the teacher.

Both words were then written on the board and copied by the children. A comparison was set up by suppositions as follows: How are you apt to feel if you sit awhile after you are tired or fatigued? Does your teacher feel *fatigued* or *tired* after her day's work? Have you ever had a tired feeling after school or after studying a long while? Did you ever hear any one say she was *exhausted?* [This word was added to the group on the board and copied when a child answered affirmatively.] What had she done to exhaust her? Was Mary exhausted awhile ago? When would you use *exhausted?* When would you use *tired?* When use *fatigued?*

The answers of the children are not given, nor the whole conversation. The children were led to observe that *fatigued* is a species of *tired*, and that *exhausted* is *tired* carried so far that a person has to stop. This was illustrated by the primitive meaning of the word.

It was not possible nor desirable at that lesson to make the meaning *fatigued* generic. The aim of the teacher was simply to have the class *perceive*, *compare*, and *classify* it. That this was probably done will be apparent to one who scrutinizes the work.

No formal statement was attempted of the truths taught in either lesson, nor was a definition essayed for any word. All proper word teaching contemplates a trial at the *use* of the word at some later period. This serves both as a review and a test of the work done.

READING.

In the primary course the pupil deals, as a rule, with words he already knows the meaning of.

At the time he learns to know the written or printed form his teacher ought to make the effort to have him assimilate a more generic meaning for each word. In addition to his lessons in learning words, which is the foundation for progress, he should also have lessons in learning phrases, such as, *on a box, into a house, to the wall.*

There are many prepositions and other such words whose meanings are not susceptible of objective illustration or of clear definition. If phrases are taught in the same way as words are, these meanings are assimilated.

The main difficulty in teaching reading has always been to get the children to comprehend the meaning of the sentences before them. This difficulty will always exist to the teacher who requires a child to *learn to read* by reading another person's thoughts. If the first year's work in reading were to be entirely of sentences of his own composition, it is believed that the load would be lifted in a great measure. Observation will convince any one that the more nearly a teacher conforms to this rule, the more easily do his pupils learn to read.

To express this principle in practical form would be to say: A child will learn to read more readily if *he makes the first series of lessons for himself.*

In reality he does this, if he learns at all, for it is manifestly impossible for one to get the author's exact thought in any case.

The product from reading a sentence to any mind is not the thought of the author, but the thought of the reader coming into the mind as an *assimilation*, from the relation of certain thought-objects, suggested by the words of the sentence, standing before him as " whole."

Unless a child has had practice in expressing relations observed, he is not prepared to analyze such relations when expressed by another. The oral expression of relations does not resemble the equivalent written or printed relation to a great enough degree for the pupil to recognize their idenity until he has made the intermediate step of formulating some of the relations *he* has observed.

To illustrate all this: Suppose the mind holds as a complex picture the following thought-objects: *A dog—a boy—chasing—a road—across (something)*—and *past time*. It is easy for that mind to compose the whole into one complex relation, and say: "The dog chased the boy across the road."

After doing this, and recognizing the written words, "the dog chased," etc., as being identical with the same words spoken, he can easily, on hearing or seeing something written *in the same idiom*, get a thought from it. The fact that children are unwittingly put to work in strange idioms, when set to practice in first readers and primers prepared by distinguished (?) authors, accounts for much of the labor expended by primary teachers.

Nothing is easier than to get children themselves to make the first lessons they are to read.

A description of the teacher's desk and the objects upon

or near it, with their relations to each other and to the desk; a narrative of the adventures they had when it rained, and they could not go out to recess; a description of a doll party in progress before them; a description of see-sawing, or some other game; in fact, all the events and scenes of home or school life are open to the teacher for selection.

But care must be taken to have the lessons as recorded for practice expressed in their *own idioms*. They must be led by degrees to express themselves in the forms used by older people. As a rule they can not get thought from sentences prepared by mature minds until they have adopted to some extent, in conversation, the habitual forms of expression belonging to maturity.

The principles thus far illustrated as applicable to primary work in teaching reading apply, with modifications, throughout the course.

1. New word-material must be introduced objectively, and at subsequent lessons the specific meanings assimilated must be made generic.

2. Lessons upon phrases and clauses and sentences must be given, alternating with the practice lessons. Repetitions of such work as has been recommended under Language serves the purpose indicated.

3. Reproduction of lessons read, or abstracts prepared in advance of lessons that are very difficult, are valuable as readings for classes.

An outline of the work contemplated by (3) is given below. The lesson selected for outline is taken from Butler's Fourth Reader. Have the children dictate the following, from inspection of the lesson if new, from memory if they have already recited it:

CHARACTERS.

a Brahmin,   a third rogue,
a rogue,   a dog,
a second rogue,   the gods.

HAPPENINGS.	TIMES.
vowing,	a certain day,
going to buy,	at same time,
inventing,	before,
questioning,	just then,
replying,	soon after,
exclaiming,	later.
protesting,	
paying,	PLACES.
sacrificing,	the market place,
smiting.	home of Brahmin.

Other groups, as MOTIVES, *to cheat, to sacrifice*, etc.; or RELATED THINGS, as *bag, pot of ghee*, etc., etc., may be added if necessary to comprehension of the "whole."

Enough questioning must be done in *what* and *how* to enable the children to get a firm mental grasp of the story.

Let them write it in character, that is, let one tell it from the standpoint of the author, another as the Brahmin, another as one of the rogues, and still another as the dog, or one of the gods.

Select meritorious efforts as matter for reading lessons. These ought to be copied on separate sheets for preservation.

GRAMMAR.

To present this subject successfully, the teacher must lead the pupil to assimilate the principles underlying constructions through his own experiences. In other words, the pupil's own sentences, or sentences made by the teacher using only words that are in the pupil's vocabulary, must be the basis for comparison.

In general, any principle of grammar may be taught by composing a group of sentences or phrases having the principle desired to be taught prominent, either as a resemblance or as a difference.

For example, suppose it is desired to prepare the pupil to understand the definition, "A noun is in the nominative case when it is the subject of a verb." Compose a group similar to the following:

    1. A boy walks.
    2. A horse walks.
    3. A man walks.
    4. A cow walks.

Question upon the details of *meaning* in these sentences and in the particular words until the pupil loses sight of the *words* that compose them. He will do this when you enable him to picture in his mind the different acts. His *perception* must be made clear. Proceed by *comparing* to discover that *boy, horse, man,* and *cow* have a common use, viz., to tell which animal *walks.*

Add others to the group, varying as below:

    5. A toad hops.
    6. A squirrel leaps.
    7. A bird flies.

By comparing these with the others, the resemblance, which still holds throughout, will assume a more generic form, thus: To tell which animal *moves.*

In the same way "which animal" may be made to assume the form, "which thing," and "moves" to take the more generic meaning, "acts."

This *case* or use of a noun needs a name, and after giving it, the pupil's crude answer to the question, "When is a noun used in the nominative case?" compared with the definition given in the text-book, will enable him to comprehend the latter.

The *same* word, used in *different* ways in a group of sentences, may be used to develop any scheme of *cases* one may wish to employ. For illustration, take the following group:

1. A *man* drank water.
2. A horse threw the *man*.
3. A *man's* hat is large.
4. A boy spoke to the *man*.
5. Joseph is a *man*.

1. Question upon the meaning (in the domain of "what") until the details are distinct and the words are lost sight of.
2. Question by comparing till the *cases* or several uses of *man* are distinct.
3. Parallel each case with a group, as follows:

1. A *man* drank water.
2. A *horse* drank water.
3. A *cow* drank water.

1. A horse threw the *man*.
2. A horse threw the *boy*.
3. A horse threw the *lady*.

1. A *man's* hat is large.
2. A *lady's* hat is large.
3. A *giant's* hat is large.

1. A boy spoke to the *man*.
2. A boy spoke to the *horse*.
2. A boy spoke to the *driver*.

1. Joseph is a *man*.
2. Henry is a *boy*.
3. Carlo is a *dog*.

And from these groups lead the pupils to *assimilate* what constitutes each case.

It is not deemed necessary to add further illustrations in this subject, as those given are a fair type of all grammar work.

GEOGRAPHY.

In this subject intellect is occupied more in perceiving than in any other process, as the number of *data* necessary to arrive at a truth are so much more numerous in most cases than in other subjects.

In general the principles that affect the life or character of a pupil are not assimilated until after the period of school life has expired. For illustration: A man is asked to leave his home and become a citizen of another country or province of his own. Now the *data* he has in reference to that country or province constitute the "whole" that contains the principle or truth which is to determine a course of so much interest to himself and family. Upon his decision rests the future happiness and prosperity of himself and those dependent on him. In like manner principles that govern investments of money, ventures in commerce, etc., etc., are all assimilated through geographical *data* which have been accumulating in the mind since early childhood.

Every human being is so related to geographical *data* that any great success in life is impossible of attainment without a comprehensive knowledge of the subject.

Its importance being paramount, then it follows that the teacher who introduces the topic to a child should adapt his work so as to prepare the pupil for assimilations that will serve him well when he needs them.

The method employed in geography should be the same as has been illustrated in Arithmetic and in Language. It should vary in detail to suit the peculiarities of the subject, these requiring more work in *perceiving* and *comparing* than in *assimilating*. There are many assimilations a pupil needs to make as he proceeds, and the teacher should cause him to make them in proper order.

"The world is my home," should be among the first assimilations made by one properly instructed in geography. This assimilation, though it may be made imperfectly at first, connects the pupil by new ties to the earth, gives him an interest in its study that will never flag through life, keeps alive his *attention*, energizes his *memory* for the Herculean task of storing away the countless *data* of this science, and rouses his *imagination* to enter upon the pleasing task of constructing that grand concept of the world that is to be the chief means of solacing his leisure hours spent in reading, that is to be the vehicle by which he may visit distant lands while quietly resting at home, and that is to bring success to his ventures in business.

The younger the children are the less apt will they be to take an interest in the study of geography from books and maps, for the reason that they have no cares upon them and do not understand the relations in which they stand to the world. As soon as they are led to comprehend that all they have, and all they will ever need to use for food, clothing, and shelter are won by hard toil from nature's stores, and that if they wish to have periods of rest and enjoyment during life they must learn nature's secrets, and be able to gain a living by a minimum of toil, they will be inspired to equip themselves for the task before them by storing up geographical knowledge.

By keeping this in mind, and by grouping the facts of the lesson so as to suggest it, even young children may be impressed by this thought.

Many *assimilations* requiring special lessons and extra time devoted to them aside from the regular text lessons are necessary to make the general work profitable in the highest degree. Such are:

(*a*) "A map is a representation of a part or the whole of the earth's surface."

(*b*) "The ocean is the great source of all life."

(*c*) "Life thrives where climate permits and where sustenance abounds."

(d) " Climate depends upon latitude, elevation, prevailing winds, and contiguous ocean currents."
(e) " Population follows natural highways."
(f) " Cities are built upon rivers or coasts."
(g) " Mines are found in mountainous sections."
(h) " Manufactories and mills are located upon streams having natural waterfalls."
(i) "An indented coast line is favorable to commerce."

A correct method in geography requires that the whole of the instruction should be founded upon, and the detached facts be learned by the light shed upon them by a series of general truths such as are given above. These are not given as a complete series, but as illustrative of the utility of such work. Thousands of facts in geography will be learned with great facility if the general truth of which each is a species is known beforehand, and these same facts will be remembered with much greater ease.

Suppose, for illustration, the following texts are encountered:*

" Arabia is chiefly a hot, desert plateau with oases of different sizes, in which dates, grapes, tamarinds, and other fruits grow. It has no general government, the inhabitants being ruled by sheiks or chiefs."

* * * * * * * * * * *

"The Empire of Japan consists of islands which contain mountains, streams, forests, and a well-cultivated soil. The principal occupations of the Japanese are agriculture, manufacturing, and mining. Its exports comprise tea, rice, silks, porcelain, fans, and lacquered ware."

* * * * * * * * * * *

"Kentucky is about half the size of Kansas. Its surface is mostly hilly, and slopes toward the northwest. The southeastern part is mountainous. In production of tobacco, hemp, and flax Kentucky surpasses every other State in the Union. The "bluegrass" region, in the basins of the Licking and Kentucky rivers, is celebrated for fine horses. Louisville, at the Falls of the Ohio River, is the most important tobacco market in the country."

---

* These extracts are copied from Barnes' Complete Geography.

PRACTICAL LESSONS. 51

A great many facts are embraced in these three extracts. The text-book from which they are taken contains nearly one hundred pages of similar matter. Is it too much to know? Can one be said to be educated in geography unless he knows much more than is given here of each of one hundred countries and important provinces? Can we expect to teach it all as detached matter?

The answers to these questions are obvious, and suggest a method founded upon *assimilations* for general principles, and patient filling in by adding to the original "wholes" from which assimilations were made the new facts as they are *perceived* after *comparing* them with the original *data*.

To illustrate the method suggested:

Suppose a class to have already assimilated the truths marked above as (*a*), (*b*), (*c*), etc., etc., would they not be much more apt to remember what is said about *Louisville*, about the *government of Arabia*, and about the *occupations* of the Japanese and their *exports?*

Is there any fact in either of the extracts that is not a species of one of the general truths given, or of some other important one in a full series? Would not a pupil so instructed, after reading what is here given, even if his text-book omitted the facts, be able to say confidently: "There are large cities in Japan, but not in Arabia?" Would he not also be able to say that Louisville is a manufacturing city, and that the people of the "bluegrass region" are wealthy, cultured, and inclined to field sports?

Are there not other facts of the countries mentioned which are indissolubly linked with those given in the extracts, and which would be readily appropriated by a mind prepared for the task?

Directions are given below as to how to prepare "wholes" for the assimilation of general truths as a basis for after-study.

1. A proper "whole" for making the assimilation, "A map is a representation of a part of the earth's surface," is the con-

struction by the pupil of one or more maps of some region or district with which he is familiar. When he has done this with the teacher's aid, and has used the same conventional signs on *his* map that are used in his text book to mark rivers, lakes, mountains, etc., he is ready to get ideas from the maps in his book.*

2. " The ocean is the great source of all life."

Take for a "whole" the elements that contribute to support life in animals and plants. Appeal to the pupils' experiences as to what terminates and prolongs life. The steps are easy to the assimilation mentioned.

3. " Life thrives where climate permits and sustenance abounds."

Take for a "whole" the cities (abodes of men) in United States, Mexico, Central America, Dominion of Canada, and (?) Greenland.

Compare as to population, etc., etc.

Ask *why* the facts are so, and the assimilation is made.

Plants and animals of different regions in North America can be compared to make the same assimilation.

4. " Cities are built upon rivers or sea-coasts."

Make a " whole" of the locations of large cities on the map of North America, and from it, by questioning, get the assimilation.

Enough examples have been given to illustrate how readily this work may be done.

The continents ought to be studied one at a time, and the principles referred to ought to be taught from the details of the first continent, as thoroughly as possible.

Such "wholes" as are given below should be used for reviews, the details to be supplied from memory by the pupils:

---

* However perfect may be the maps of a text-book, they will not suffice to illustrate fully such texts as have been quoted above. Relief maps of continents are a necessity for the best instruction. These can be made by a teacher, using paper pulp or putty, or some other plastic material for the elevations. Fine maps of this character are now made for sale.

CUBA.

Gulf of Mexico—Florida—Spain—Havana—Matanzas—oranges—lemons—tobacco—sugar—mahogany—rosewood—Columbus—1492—hurricanes—Spaniards—Negroes, etc., etc.

After these details are arrived at, the general direction being, "Put down what *Cuba* makes you think of"—as a class exercise—and arranged logically, have the class write up the geography of the island.

These "wholes" may be made of many topics, as *Amazon, Andes, cotton, rice, coal, Caucasian race,* etc. They serve admirably to put knowledge in a classified form into the memory.

Many new words are brought into the vocabulary by the study of geography. The requirements of Postulate IV, as well as illustrations under Reading in this Monograph, make it certain that a teacher should have the geography *read* by the pupils, and not recited from memory, as was the universal method not many years ago. In other words, there ought to be no reciting of answers with books closed, and maps hid, except in review lessons, illustrated above.

ETHICS.

At the foundation of right doing lies right thinking. Every member of society stands in certain relations to his fellows, and certain duties are incumbent on him. These duties are two-fold, viz., To individuals and to the whole.

To fulfill any duty marks a man as possessing the virtue that is its fulfillment. *Honesty* is a virtue that will inhere in any individual who respects the property-rights of others. And so for all virtues. Now is it important to instruct young persons in ethics? And can it be done without teaching the tenets of any church?

No one who has observed the growth of the money-getting

feeling in this country, who has observed its ruthless hand corrupting legislation, defiling religion, and grinding poverty, can for a moment deny that something ought to be done to rescue us from that state into which we are drifting, a state in which the only tie that shall bind us is that weak one known as "honor among thieves."

The church, or rather churches, of the land ought to see to it, while they have the power over public opinion, that ethics is introduced and taught in the common schools. This is the only means by which all classes can be reached. No other influence extends to every home in the land.

The necessity for teaching ethics being apparent, and the medium through which enlightenment is to come provided, it only remains to agree upon the curriculum and the method.

No church prejudices can be offended if the teachers make the dictionary the basis of their work. By this simple means all contentions can be quieted, and the good work of training the youth of our land morally, be consummated.

Man, "created in God's image," is a progressive being, and inherits a tendency to admire the *beautiful*, to recognize the *true*, and to retain the *good*. If noble ideals are placed before him, and connected with his daily walk, he will strive to reach them and gradually realize them.

The experiences of a race in conduct record themselves in the vocabulary of that race in the names for virtues and vices. Now, if the teacher will but give lessons upon these abstract terms, he will be laying the foundation for correct conduct. If the same pains were taken in school to acquaint the children with the meanings of *honesty* and *fortitude* as are taken to teach *exponent* and *predicate nominative*, the results in ethics would be similar to the results in science.

Postulate IV assumes that words must be made generic in meaning to the child to be in any high degree useful to him. Now, to make any word generic in mind, its full range of meaning must be brought to consciousness, and comparison

PRACTICAL LESSONS. 55

ıat approach it in meaning,
ıosite in meaning.
aching the virtue expressed
below.

ORTITUDE.

ld,
and
nder financial reverses.
ɔh,
ıd
, of a limb.
rs. Garfield, Joan d' Arc,
imozin, Jesus Christ, Casabi-

read to the class. Compare
courage, bravery, endurance,
rs possessing like qualities.
imidity, hesitation. fear, treach-
ualities.
early every case a pupil will
ne a man or woman of forti-
, almost certainly, to assimi-
f the teacher will but take
imples of *fortitude* that have
f he can bring these to the
ibited in their own conduct,
hanging the current of their

any word are necessary, and
ι lasting impression.
ples observed by them, and if
on the subject of any lesson,
ı that they have learned the
begin to exhibit in their con-

ANDREW J. RICKOFF, LL. D., author Arithmetics, Readers, etc. New York.

I have read almost every paragraph, and many of them three or four times. You are certainly right, mainly, if not entirely. You have made a valuable contribution to the many excellent books on Pedagogics, with which we are favored from almost every direction. I think it would pay you—it would certainly do great good—if you were to put the work into more permanent form, if you would extend the treatment of your *postulates* and multiply your illustrations.

I am especially well pleased with the clearness with which you have set forth your theory, and heartily agree with every word you say under that head.

feeling in this country, wh
corrupting legislation, defili
can for a moment deny thai
rescue us from that state ir
in which the only tie that
known as " honor among th

The church, or rather chu
it, while they have the pow
is introduced and taught i
the only means by which i
other influence extends to e

The necessity for teachir
medium through which enl
it only remains to agree
method.

No church prejudices car
the dictionary the basis o
means all contentions can b
training the youth of our la

Man, " created in God's
and inherits a tendency to t
the *true*, and to retain the g
before him, and connected
to reach them and gradually

The experiences of a race
the vocabulary of that race i
Now, if the teacher will l
stract terms, he will be layir
duct. If the same pains we:
children with the meanings
taken to teach *exponent* and
in ethics would be similar to

Postulate IV assumes tha
meaning to the child to be i
Now, to make any word ge
meaning must be brought

of it must be made with others that approach it in meaning, and with others still that are opposite in meaning.

An outline of a "whole" for teaching the virtue expressed by the word *Fortitude* is presented below.

EXAMPLES OF FORTITUDE.

(*a*) A woman burying her child,
(*b*) Sending her son to battle, and
(*c*) Comforting her husband under financial reverses.
(*d*) A soldier on a forced march,
(*e*) Confronting the enemy, and
(*f*) Suffering the amputation of a limb.
(*g*) Historical examples: Mrs. Garfield, Joan d' Arc, Washington, Marshal Ney, Guatimozin, Jesus Christ, Casabianca, etc., etc.

Let these examples be told or read to the class. Compare them with examples of *strength, courage, bravery, endurance, resoluteness, persistence,* and others possessing like qualities. Compare also with examples of *timidity, hesitation, fear, treachery,* and others having opposite qualities.

If this work is well done, in nearly every case a pupil will be inspired with a desire to become a man or woman of fortitude. Moreover, he may be led, almost certainly, to assimilate a principle for guidance, if the teacher will but take pains to add to the "whole" examples of *fortitude* that have been exhibited by children. If he can bring these to the memory of the children, as exhibited in their own conduct, he is almost sure to succeed in changing the current of their lives.

Repetitions of the work with any word are necessary, and also tests in order to be sure of a lasting impression.

If pupils can point out examples observed by them, and if they can construct an essay upon the subject of any lesson, no better evidence can be given that they have learned the meaning of the term. If they begin to exhibit in their conduct an example of a virtue taught them, it is proof positive that they have assimilated a rule for action.

NOTE.—The manner of giving such lessons as has been outlined here, is more elaborately treated under *Character Education*. The nature and value of the "Hypothetical Discourse" in teaching right conduct is there illustrated fully.

ALGEBRA.

The authors understand that what is written here concerning algebra is but part of arithmetic. Hence it ought to be taught as such and at the same time with arithmetic. The use of a letter to represent *any* number seems as simple as the use of any class name, and is as easily learned by the average pupil.

In the review of Principle (2) of Arithmetic (see page 24), the use of *any* number of things as a unit should be made very familiar to the pupil. There he learns that

3, 4 sts. + 5, 4 sts. + 6, 4 sts. = 14, 4 sts.

Such examples as:

5, 3 sts. + 6, 5 sts. + 5, 8 sts. + 5, 9 sts. = ?

should be given the pupil, expecting him to apply Principle 10 (see page 24), and write:

3, 5 sts. + 6, 5 sts. + 8, 5 sts. + 9, 5 sts. = 26, 5 sts.

The units and coefficients should finally reach up into the thousands. The transition to

3, a sts. + 6, a sts. + 8, a sts. + 9, a sts. = 26 a sts.,

is simple and is easily made. To this end vary the number of things in the unit while the coefficients remain the same; thus by resemblances disclosing the same demand for a class name for the number of things in the unit as for any object, as chair.

The use of this method in subtraction, as in Principle 11 (see page 25), will familiarize the pupil with the use of letters as names for *any* number.

In arriving at Principle 10^I (see page 24), the following steps are safe. By Principle 10; 6, 12 sts. = 12, 6 sts., omit

PRACTICAL LESSONS. 57

ting the things $6 \cdot 12 = 12 \cdot 6$ (1). So, also, 3, 2 sts. $= 2, 3$ sts., omitting the things $3 \cdot 2 = 2 \cdot 3$. So, also, 3, 4 sts. $= 4, 3$ sts., $3 \cdot 4 = 4 \cdot 3$. Substitute in (1) and we have:

$3 \cdot 2 \cdot 3 \cdot 4 = 4 \cdot 3 \cdot 2 \cdot 3 = 4 \cdot 2 \cdot 3 \cdot 3$, etc. Doing likewise with 4 and we have: $3 \cdot 2 \cdot 3 \cdot 2 \cdot 2 = 2 \cdot 2 \cdot 2 \cdot 3 \cdot 3 = 72$. Having, by repetitions, established Principle 10', then exercise the class thoroughly thus: What and how many prime factors are in 12? in 8? in 17? in 54? etc. Speak of 8 as having three 2's as factors; of 12 as having two 2's and one 3 as factors, etc. Ask at the same time for the number of 2's as units in 8, in 12, etc. Write on the board $2 + 2 + 2 + 2 = 4$, 2's $= 8$, and $2 \cdot 2 \cdot 2 = 8$. Do the same with 12, 16, 24, etc. If the attention of the pupil is called to use of 4 in 4, 2's, and the question asked, why not use a figure to express the number of 2's as factors in 8, 16, 32, etc., pupils find no difficulty in appreciating the need, and are prepared for $2 \cdot 2 \cdot 2 = 2^3 = 8$, etc. Now ask for the *factors* of the product of 12 and 24 *without* knowing the product, and pupils easily write $12 \cdot 24 = 2 \cdot 2 \cdot 3 \times 2 \cdot 2 \cdot 2 \cdot 3$, and applying Principle 10', we have $12 \cdot 24 = 2 \cdot 2 \cdot 2 \cdot 2 \cdot 3 \cdot 3 = 2^4 \cdot 3^2$; with which result parallel $12 + 24 = 6$, 2's $+ 12$, 2's $= 18$, 2's, and $12 \cdot 24 = 2^2 \cdot 3 \times 2^3 \cdot 3 = 2^5 \cdot 3^2$, and the average pupil has discovered for himself the principle that exponents of like factors are added in multiplication. Place on the board such examples as:

$$24 \times 36 \times 72 \times 96 \times 48 \times 144 = ?$$

and ask for the factors of the product without finding it. On the board, after pupils find it, write:

$24 \times 36 \times 72 \times 96 \times 48 \times 144 = 2^{21} \cdot 3^9$.
$2^3 \cdot 3 \times 2^2 \cdot 3^2 \times 2^3 \cdot 3^2 \times 2^5 \cdot 3 \times 2^4 \cdot 3 \times 2^4 \cdot 3^2$.

Then:

$$a^6 b^7 c^8 d^3 \times a^2 b^5 d^4 \times a^5 c^6 d^8 \times c^7 d^4 = ?$$

and others. Then:

$$a^{64} b^{78} \times a^{96} b^{49} = ?$$
$$a^{364} c^{565} \times a^{468} b^{796} = ?$$

and others of like kind, ending the group with $a^m b^n \times a^p b^q = ?$ and after a little repetition nearly all will readily do such examples as:

$$a^{m+n} b^{p+s+2} \times a^{2m+r} b^{p+q} = ?$$

Then give such a group as follows:

$$a^{99} b^{199} \times ab = ?$$
$$a^{569} b^{999} \times ab = ?$$

and others, ending with $a^m b^n \times ab = ?$ and a majority will be able to work the last example. The greatest care must be exercised throughout the whole of such work to *let* the pupil discover for himself the results, and how as well as why it is so. It is not necessary to call the attention of the reader to the application of the various postulates in the work given here.

In order to lead the pupil to discover for himself the multiplication of polynomials the following "whole" is suggested: Let the pupil multiply 46 by 68, and then put on the board as he answers the various questions: "What are the parts of 46?" "What are the parts of 68?" etc.

```
46=         40+ 6=                       2²·10+2 ·3
68=         60+ 8=                       2·3 ·10+   2³
───         ──────                       ──────────
368=        320+48=                      + 2⁵·10+2⁴·3
276 =2400+360      =2³·3·10²+2²·3²·10
─────────────────────────────────────────────────────
3128=2400+680+48=2³·3·10²+2²·3²·10 + 2⁵·10+2⁴·3
```

A few repetitions of this "whole" will enable the pupil to work with ease such examples as:

$$(a^m b^n + a^r b^c) \times (a^p b^q + a b^c) = ?$$

It will be observed that the use of the "10," as above indicated, will gain two ends, viz: (1) Make the pupil familiar with the scale of tens, and (2) make the teaching of division of polynomials easy.

In order to enable the pupil to arrive at the meaning of $a^{\frac{m}{n}}$ proceed thus: Ask what does $\frac{2}{3}$, 12 mean? Pupil answers,

PRACTICAL LESSONS. 59

Separate "12" into three equal *parts*, and take two of these *parts* as units. $12 = 4 + 4 + 4 \therefore \frac{2}{3}$, $12 = 4 + 4 = 2$, 4's $= 8$. Then ask: "What does $8^{\frac{2}{3}}$ mean?" A few pupils answer immediately without any repetition, Separate 8 into three equal *factors*, and take two of them as *factors*. Repetition will enable nearly all pupils to arrive at same result. Place on board after pupils have solved them:

$$8^{\frac{2}{3}} = 2^2 \quad : 16^{\frac{3}{4}} = 2^3 \quad : \text{etc.}$$
$$8 = 2 \cdot 2 \cdot 2 : 16 = 2 \cdot 2 \cdot 2 \cdot 2 : \text{etc.}$$

and ask what $a^{\frac{m}{n}}$ means. To assure results write $a = b^n$ and $b^m = c$, and ask pupils what $a^{\frac{m}{n}}$ equals. Use such examples as:

$$2^{3 \cdot \frac{3}{2}} = ? \quad (2^3)^{\frac{3}{2}} = ? \quad \left(2^{3^{\frac{3}{2}}}\right) = ? \quad \text{freely.}$$

Teaching division of monomials is an easy matter. Space forbids details; the results arrived at below will indicate processes. Remember, *pupils* must arrive at results for themselves. Ask pupils to find all the exact divisors of 12 by the *use of factors*, and when they have done the work place on the board as follows, calling attention to the names of the parts:

	Divisor.	Quotient.		Multiplicand.	Multiplier
Dividend.	2	$= 2 \cdot 3$		2	$\times 2 \cdot 3$
$12 \div$	$2 \cdot 2$	$= 3$	Product.	$2 \cdot 2$	$\times 3$
$2 \cdot 2 \cdot 3$	$2 \cdot 3$	$= 2$	$12 =$	$2 \cdot 3$	$\times 2$
	3	$= 2 \cdot 2$		3	$\times 2 \cdot 2$
	$2 \cdot 2 \cdot 3$	$= 1$		$2 \cdot 2 \cdot 3$	$\times 1$

Then ask pupils to do likewise with 24, 36, etc. Then place on the board such examples as:

$$2^3 \cdot 3^4 \cdot 5^7 \div \begin{cases} 2^2 \cdot 3 \cdot 5^2 = ? \\ 2^3 \cdot 3^2 \cdot 5^3 = ? \\ 3^3 \cdot 5^7 = ? \\ 2^3 \cdot 3^4 \cdot 5^7 = ? \\ 5^7 = ? \end{cases} \quad 2^3 \cdot 3^4 \cdot 5^7 = \begin{cases} 2^2 \cdot 3 \cdot 5^2 \times ? \\ 2^3 \cdot 3^2 \cdot 5^3 \times ? \\ 3^3 \cdot 5^7 \times ? \\ 2^3 \cdot 3^4 \cdot 5^7 \times ? \\ 5^7 \times ? \end{cases}$$

After repetition with figures use letters freely both as factors and exponents.

To teach division of polynomials, reverse process of teaching multiplication.

In subtraction, after pupils have read up their notes on the subject, give them two numbers, such as 57 and 96, and let the pupils compare them as found in their notes. After repetition, if necessary, put on the board as follows:

$(+96) - (+57) = +39 \qquad (+a) - (+b) = ?$
$(+96) - (-57) = +153 \qquad (+a) - (-b) = ?$
$(-96) - (+57) = -153 \qquad (-a) - (+b) = ?$
$(-96) - (-57) = -39 \qquad (-a) - (-b) = ?$
$(+57) - (+96) = -39 \qquad (+b) - (+a) = ?$
$(+57) - (-96) = +153 \qquad (+b) - (-a) = ?$
$(-57) - (+96) = -153 \qquad (-b) - (+a) = ?$
$(-57) - (-96) = +39 \qquad (-b) - (-a) = ?$

and require pupils to write answers in parentheses thus: $+(a-b)$, $+(a+b)$, $-(a+b)$, etc., having informed them that the number "a" is greater than the number "b." Some pupils will do the work without difficulty. Repetition with large numbers will call the attention of the pupils to what they do and how they do it. If, then, a few pupils remain who have not succeeded, by questioning in the *what*, *how*, and *why*, the teacher will enable all, or nearly all, to do the work by themselves.

Announcing the proposition that John has five debts less of six dollars each than James, and requesting the pupil to compare John to James, will enable him to discover that the product of -5 and -6 is $+30$.

Let the pupil be led to make the following "whole," and he learns when trinomials can be separated into two binomial factors, and how to do it:

$42 \times 43 = (4 \cdot 10 + 2)(4 \cdot 10 + 3) = 4^2 \cdot 10^2 + 5 \cdot 4 \cdot 10 + 6$
$54 \times 56 = (5 \cdot 10 + 4)(5 \cdot 10 + 6) = 5^2 \cdot 10^2 + 10 \cdot 5 \cdot 10 + 24$
$78 \times 79 = (7 \cdot 10 + 8)(7 \cdot 10 + 9) = 7^2 \cdot 10^2 + 17 \cdot 7 \cdot 10 + 72$

When three or four of these are done, ask pupils to use *letters*, and if they fail, ask them to observe closely what they do and how they do it, and continue:

$61 \times 67 = (6 \cdot 10 + 1)(6 \cdot 10 + 7) = 6^2 \cdot 10^2 + 8 \cdot 6 \cdot 10 + 7$
$39 \times 33 = (3 \cdot 10 + 9)(3 \cdot 10 + 3) = 3^2 \cdot 10^2 + 12 \cdot 3 \cdot 10 + 27$

Then many pupils will generalize thus:

$$(a \cdot 10 + b)(a \cdot 10 + c) = a^2 10^2 + (b + c) a \cdot 10 + bc.$$

Those who fail can generally be brought by questioning in detail as to what, how, and why to reach the desired result. Then put x for 10 and get:

$$(ax + b)(ax + c) = a^2 x^2 + (b + c) ax + bc.$$

In applying this result proceed as follows: place on the board

$$a^2 x^2 + 10\, ax + \left\{ \begin{array}{l} = \\ = \\ = \\ = \\ = \end{array} \right.$$

and request the class to find third terms, and factor resulting polynomials. Some will do this work without any more teaching. With others, for relation of 10 and the third term, call attention to $b + c$ and bc in the general expression, and lead them to do as follows:

$$10 = \left\{ \begin{array}{l} 9 + 1 \\ 8 + 2 \\ 7 + 3 \\ 6 + 4 \\ 5 + 5 \\ \tfrac{11}{2} + \tfrac{9}{2} \end{array} \right. \text{ and } \left. \begin{array}{l} 9 \times 1 = 9 \\ 8 \times 2 = 16 \\ 7 \times 3 = 21 \\ 6 \times 4 = 24 \\ 5 \times 5 = 25 \\ \tfrac{11}{2} \times \tfrac{9}{2} = \tfrac{99}{4} \end{array} \right\} \text{The third terms desired.}$$

Then after the same manner place on the board:

$$a^2 x^2 + \left\{ \begin{array}{c} \\ \\ \\ \end{array} \right\} ax + 36 = \left\{ \begin{array}{c} \\ \\ \\ \end{array} \right.$$

and ask pupils to supply coefficients of second term, and factor the results. A few repetitions serve to familiarize the pupil with the work.

Put on a table two piles of 40 straws each, and let the class write up on their pads, verifying the result by inspection of the straws:

$$2, 40 \text{ sts.} = 80 \text{ sts.}$$

Then opposite each pile place two piles of 19 each, with 2 straws to the left of each pair of 19's. Then lead the pupils to write up the result as follows, verifying as before:

$$2 (2 \text{ sts.} + 2, 19 \text{ sts.}) = 80 \text{ sts.}$$

Then with other straws, for each 19 arrange three piles of 5 straws each with a pile of 4 to the left of each group of three 5's. As before lead the pupil in verifying and writing up, as follows:

$$2 [2 \text{ sts.} + 2 (4 \text{ sts.} + 3, 5 \text{ sts.})] = 80 \text{ sts.}$$

With another 80 straws make an arrangement based on the last result by separating the 5's into piles of 3 and 2, and arrive at the following arrangement of straws:

$$| | \left\{ \begin{array}{l} | | | | \left\{ \begin{array}{l} | | |\ \ | | \\ | | |\ \ | | \\ | | |\ \ | | \end{array} \right. \\ | | | | \left\{ \begin{array}{l} | | |\ \ | | \\ | | |\ \ | | \\ | | |\ \ | | \end{array} \right. \end{array} \right. \quad | | \left\{ \begin{array}{l} | | | | \left\{ \begin{array}{l} | | |\ \ | | \\ | | |\ \ | | \\ | | |\ \ | | \end{array} \right. \\ | | | | \left\{ \begin{array}{l} | | |\ \ | | \\ | | |\ \ | | \\ | | |\ \ | | \end{array} \right. \end{array} \right.$$

Pupils when asked will generally succeed in writing up the result, which is as follows:

$$2 \left\{ 2 \text{ sts.} + 2 [4 \text{ sts.} + 3 (3 \text{ sts.} + 2 \text{ sts.})] \right\} = 80 \text{ sts.}$$

If any fail to do so repetitions will assure success.

Continue in repetitions by making arrangements of straws that will give such results as follows:

$$3 \left\{ 2 \text{ sts.} + 2 [3 \text{ sts.} + 5 (4 \text{ sts.} + 1 \text{ st.})] \right\} = 174 \text{ sts.}$$

Reverse the process by giving a parenthetical expression, thus:

$$2\left(3\text{ sts.}+2\left\{4\text{ sts.}+2\left[5\text{ sts.}+3\left(2\text{ sts.}+3\text{ sts.}\right)\right]\right\}\right) = 182\text{ sts.}$$

And require the pupils to arrange the straws to correspond.

GEOMETRY.

The intention in these remarks on teaching geometry is only to introduce the subject and indicate the manner of application of the postulates.

Prepare a number of similar rectangles cut out of pasteboard. Give each pupil three or four of these rectangles, and one *not* similar to them. The three or four similar rectangles constitute a "whole." The pupil is expected (1) to discover in what respects they resemble each other; (2) to discover the principle, a content of these resemblances, that "Rectangles whose sides are equimultiples, when placed on each other properly, will have their free corners in the same straight line." It would be well to have a five-sided figure in full view of the class. Pupils will generally write, in effect, as follows: "These four pieces of pasteboard resemble in having four sides, four square corners, and in being longer than they are wide. They differ in the lengths of their sides." A few questions in the *what* will develop in their minds that they resemble in having opposite sides the same length, and equally distant apart at the ends. Ask the pupils to place the rectangles cornering together on each other, and the fact that the free corner of the dissimilar one is out by itself will call their attention to the fact that the three similar rectangles have *their* free corners in the same line, which they will verify with their rulers, and announce that the three rectangles resemble in "pointing in the same direction."

Take the odd rectangle from them and ask them to reduce the three, by scales given, to the same size on their pads, when they will discover the idea that their sides are equimultiples.

Then ask the pupils to make a number of rectangles on their pads with sides equimultiples. Some will do this by drawing the diagonal of the large rectangle and make the others corner on it. Others will take two numbers, find the equimultiples, and construct the rectangles.

Now ask them to discover how many times a smaller rectangle is contained in a larger, and they will generally do the work with ease. Then, by comparing results in numbers with the corresponding common multiplier, they discover that the former is the square of the latter. Ask them to explain why this is so, and they will answer, that the multiplier tells how many of the smaller rectangles can be constructed in the larger each way, the product of which numbers gives the whole number of the smaller contained in the larger, because the number in a row multiplied by the number of rows will give the whole number. Now call their attention to the fact that the square of any number is contained in the square of any multiple of that number, a number of times represented by the square of the multiplier; or, referring to figures prepared on the board, show the same thing between the base of the smaller rectangle and its multiple, the base of the larger rectangle, and they arrive at the principle that "The ratio of similar rectangles is the ratio of the squares on corresponding sides."

Ask them for the number of square inches in a rectangle, and few pupils fail to answer: "Multiply the number of inches in length by the number of inches in width." Then they can readily be led to disvover the principle that "The ratio of similar rectangles is the ratio of the squares," from the fact that areas are products of bases and altitudes, the common multiplier entering as a factor in both length and width.

Give each pupil a rectangle and a parallelogram of equal bases and altitudes (a "whole"), and ask for resemblances and differences, and the average pupil will readily discover the equality of areas among other resemblances. A few questions will enable all to discover that fact.

PRACTICAL LESSONS. 65

Give each pupil three similar parallelograms cut out of pasteboard, and they will readily discover the resemblances and differences as they did with the rectangles, etc.

Give the pupils similar right triangles cut out of pasteboard, and by use of rectangles they readily discover relations and areas, etc.

Give the pupils similar obtuse angled triangles, and they readily discover the facts as above.

The serious difficulties of the pupils begin with the attempt to discover the three bases and their altitudes of one obtuse angled triangle.* By standing the triangle on any base they find the corresponding altitude, but are confused by the figure. A little patience with three separate triangles will enable them to apply the principle so as to find the area of one obtuse angled triangle in the three modes.

THE ANGLE.

It is hardly necessary to premise that a pupil must know what "direction" is in order to understand the "difference of two directions," which is an angle.

Ask all the pupils to point at some object in the room, and then to write up what they were doing. Then ask every pupil to point in the direction that object is from where he sits, and let them "write up" that act also. Then, pointing in some direction, ask all to point in the same direction that you are pointing, and write up that also.

Mark two points on the board, and ask one pupil to make an arrow pointing from one to the other point, and another pupil at the same time to make an arrow from the second point to the first, and ask all to write up.

Secure a number of long pointers; call up a number of boys and let them point now at this object and now at that, and then in any indicated direction. Place two boys wide

---
* Some pupils overcome this difficulty by constructing the three parallelograms, of which the triangle is half, and finding the three bases and altitudes through the three parallelograms.

apart with pointers; ask them to point in the same direction. Call up a third and fourth to point in the same direction. Ask: "Are these all the same direction, or are they only pointing in the same direction?"

Make a number of points on the board, and let one pupil elect a direction for his arrow; then let pupil after pupil make arrows from other points in the same direction; then ask a number of pupils in different parts of the room to give the same direction with pointers. Ask, again, if these represent the same direction or are only pointing in the same direction.

Starting with a clean board, make an arrow diagonally up on the board, and ask each pupil to do the same on his pad. Name the arrow A, with letter at the point. Then draw another arrow as distant as practicable in the same direction; ask pupils to do likewise, and ask pupils to name this direction. Certainly all who put A at its point understand the matter. Then put A at its point on the board. Some inches away from the first arrow draw a second, making an angle with A, and when pupils have done likewise, ask for a name. Put B at its point and draw another arrow in the same direction some feet away, and name as before. So continue until you have on the board and the pupils have on their pads a number of arrows in each of a number of directions. Ask pupils which direction, B or C, differs more from A. After a little exercise in this matter, ask pupils how to make it evident that C differs more from A in direction than B does. Some pupil will suggest taking a point and drawing three arrows in directions of A, B, and C. Continue this exercise until pupils are familiar with the idea of difference of two directions and begin to call it "angle."

Ask all your pupils to point at you, and then ask them to think that you are pointing at every one of them, and write up facts as to resemblances and differences of directions. Some will use the word "opposite." Some will say: "You are pointing just the other way from that in which I am pointing." Use the words "opposite directions," and apply them to the case in hand.

Place four boys, A, B, C, and D, in different parts of the room; ask A and B to point at each other, and ask C to point in a direction opposite to the direction in which A is pointing, and D to point in direction opposite to the one in which B is pointing. Then ask some pupil to use a pointer and point in a direction midway between these opposite directions. He will probably try to get midway between the four boys, but if you have the four boys properly located he will find that impossible. Then write on the board the two propositions, viz: "Place your person midway between the pupils," and "point in a direction midway between the opposite directions." Ask for resemblances and differences. When satisfactory answers are received, ask the pupils at their seats, without leaving their seats, to point in a direction midway between the opposite directions. A number will do this for you without delay, and if you give out six pointers, you will have six different directions which are midway between the given opposite directions. Then take four points on the blackboard at considerable distances from each other, name them A, B, C, and D. Ask some pupil to put an arrow with its point at A; a second pupil to put an arrow with its point at B, pointing in opposite directions from that at A; a third pupil to place an arrow with its point at C, pointing in opposite direction from the arrow at A; and likewise place an arrow at D in the opposite direction from that at B. Let pupils write up *what* and *how*, and then give out pointers to different pupils to give direction midway between these opposites, and then let a number of pupils draw arrows at different points, E, F, G, etc., pointing in directions midway between the opposites that are on the board. Then the pupils are prepared for the name, *right angle*.

With this unit, they should be required to actually measure a number of acute and obtuse angles. This measurement of angles with a right angle for a unit is readily taught by the methods of this Monograph.

Ask the pupils to draw a triangle like one on the board, which the teacher makes obtuse angled. Ask the pupils to separate it into its parts. The average pupil will readily find the six parts. Ask him to construct another triangle with any three of the six parts. He will probably not select the three angles; if he does, resemblances and differences will disclose the facts in the case, as it does whatever three parts he may select. Then let him select three other parts, and construct another triangle, and so continue; the teacher always asking for resemblance and difference between the resulting triangle and the one he started with, until he is perfectly familiar with the evident principle in the case. Of course, when he happens to select two sides and an angle opposite one of the sides, he may have a result, well known to the reader, which must be treated as correct principles in teaching demand.

With older pupils it requires some four weeks, an hour each day, to do this work well; with younger pupils, some ten weeks. Older pupils at this stage ought to have now and then a proposition to study, as found in the average geometry of the day. The teacher ought to write on the board such a demonstration for the younger pupils to copy on their pads and study under the teacher's directions, with the *what*, *how*, and *why* while writing the propositions.

It seems sure that all of geometry can be taught after the same plan, but it has been found that pupils use books in a satisfactory manner after this period.

NOTE.—The observant teacher will perceive that all the principles of arithmetic (pages 24 and 25) apply to geometry.

Principles (13) and (14) in geometry take the following forms, viz:

$$\left. \begin{array}{l} A \propto B \\ A' \propto B' \end{array} \right\} \therefore \begin{array}{l} A \div A' = B \div B' \therefore \\ A : A' = B : B'. \end{array}$$

and

$$\left. \begin{array}{l} B \propto \frac{1}{C} \\ B' \propto \frac{1}{C'} \end{array} \right\} \therefore \begin{array}{l} B \div B' = C' \div C \therefore \\ B : B' = C' : C. \end{array}$$

PRACTICAL LESSONS. 69

Also an additional principle appears in this connection, which may be generically stated thus:

$$A \propto \left\{ \begin{array}{c} B \\ C \\ \text{etc.} \\ \frac{1}{D} \\ \frac{1}{E} \\ \text{etc.} \end{array} \right\} \therefore A = \frac{B \cdot C \text{ etc.}}{D \cdot E \text{ etc.}} \times (\text{some constant*}).$$

---

*This constant must be used in the generic expression.

EDUCATION OF CHARACTER.

What a man does once under given circumstances does not proclaim his character; but if he does any one thing repeatedly under like circumstances, that one act may be regarded as a phenomenon of his character. If a boy habitually comes into the school-room when the bell rings, we credit him with *promptness* as one element of his character. And so, every *habit* of the individual is a mark of his character.

If a man gives habitually, as calls are made upon him, he must be credited with *liberality*. His failing to give at any one time does not invalidate the previous estimate. Moreover, a man does not sit in judgment upon his own acts; the standard of right action is fixed by public opinion; it changes from age to age. Just now, for us, it has its foundation in the precepts of Christ, and he who does his duty faithfully must conform his teaching to that standard. Now, do not these facts lead inevitably to the conclusion that he who succeeds in molding character aright must fix habits of action that to the world indicate excellence in character?

A man's whole life is spent in accomplishing ends through means. If all the ends he seeks are good, and all the means employed by him are right, then his character is perfect.

Now, certain ends, as *food, clothing,* etc., demand a large share of every one's energies and time for their accomplishment. Satisfying them becomes in fact the *business* of his life. For gaining these constant ends, by comparing the means that he has from time to time employed, he assimilates certain principles. These laws as constant means control to a great extent his habits and develop his character.

The ends one shall seek are suggested by his feelings; these command his Will and it obeys; he seeks the suggested ends;

his *experiences* commence. Certain ends accomplished, or means employed bring him into conflict with his environment, and he experiences pain where he anticipated pleasure. Now his Intellect begins its benign work; he makes a rule for himself in each case of experienced pain; his Intellect gives a lesson to his emotional nature.

But Emotion again prompts him, and again his Will obeys. Again his environment inflicts pain, and as his promptings must have been stronger than at first to overcome his determination, so his persistence is greater. His Intellect, this time starting from principle, can make its lesson more forcible.

As often as this conflict may be waged, just so often is the end the same. The determination dictated by the intellect will become *generic*, and a *habit* be born.

Passion, in some cases, may temporarily or permanently control the Will, but the individual ever remembers the lessons of his Intellect, and despises himself when disobeying its mandates.

Those habits which are acquired through a triumph of the intellect over the emotional nature are *good*, because they are founded on truth, the assimilation of which is the work proper of the intellect. *Bad* habits are acquired by obeying the emotional nature. Such are observed to prevail with peoples and individuals whose intellects are naturally weak, or who have been so unfortunate as to have had meager intellectual training.

The problem to be solved by the teacher or the parent who undertakes to educate the character of a young person is: *To prepare him to so act as to be in harmony with an ever-varying environment.*

The pupil's character will be educated aright if he acquires good habits and drops such bad habits as he may have fallen into. Good habits are at war with bad habits, and, if the teacher will but re-enforce the good in the struggle, their victory will be more certain.

Fault-finding, lecturing, and scolding are among the worst

means a teacher can employ to cure bad habits, for the very apparent reason that the pupil does not realize that the fault-finding is directed, not at his person but at his habit; he infers that his teacher does not love him, and this impression puts the teacher outside of the pupil's environment for good, and makes his influence a nullity or an actual evil.

Good habits must be cultivated systematically, and herein lies the solution of the problem. What are the elements of that solution, what are the laws that should govern the teacher? The objective point for the teacher is to lead the pupil to form *generic* determinations.* As has already been indicated, the making of these generic determinations are the turning-points in life. Victor Hugo said: "A tuft of sod against which a soldier rests his heel in the conflict may decide the fate of a nation."

So, a little thing may often mar or make a character. A "word in season" by his teacher may turn a boy from the downward path, or by a single mistake in judgment that teacher may start him on the road to ruin. Every person of mature years can recall many such turning-points in his life. They abide in memory with peculiar force, because each of them marks a triumph of temptation, or a victory for truth, the very sap upon which the intellect feeds.

Now, can these determinations and their resulting good habits be *made* to come to pass with any certainty, or must we regard them as providential entirely?

As a teacher's wisdom may decide in answering this question, so will his practice be shaped. If he believes that Providence alone determines, he will leave the issue in His hands; if the teacher believes that *he* is one instrument of Providence for the well-being of his pupil, he will feel called on to work as well as pray.

---

* By a generic determination is meant a resolution to act *at all times* and *in all places* according to the dictates of the law conceived to be proper. There is a difference between determining to quit wine and determining to quit all intoxicating liquors; between resolving to be prompt to-morrow and to be prompt every day: the one is particular, the other generic.

There are certain conditions in this problem of educating character which are *constant*. Success can in no case be certain unless these are satisfied, viz:

1. Every pupil has an environment which differs more or less from that of every other pupil.
2. The pupil's intellect is a part of his own environment.
3. The teacher must know the environment of each pupil.
4. The teacher must know himself as he is.*

The teacher must know the particular environment of each pupil in order to put into it good influences that are lacking, and to take out bad influences that are present.

What will produce good results with one will often produce the contrary results with another; what is needed to influence one is already in another's environment, or if put there would do no good. A boy who loves music can be benefited by it; one who loves it not fails to be influenced by it. The "I do not like that" of a person that he respects causes a child to pause; where respect is wanting he does not often heed it. A teacher once had occasion to lecture a lad about something he had done. "I wish you would ask your Uncle Will what he thinks about such an offense," he ventured as a feeler. The boy responded, with a blush, "I will, but don't you tell him first. Let *me* tell him." That teacher had found a new element to put in that boy's environment; his desire to retain his Uncle Will's love became a disciplinary force with the boy from that day.

Tom Brown needed the gentle influence of the pastor's son upon his rugged nature; he needed care as a burden in his life to discipline him; the little timid boy needed a manly

---

* This condition can be understood by reading carefully Christ's qualifications as a teacher as outlined in Hebrews ii, 17-18; iv, 15, and those of Paul in 1st Corinthians, ix, 19 to 22.

protector; the wise Arnold brought them together. It was a simple thing to do, but it produced a great change in the life of each. This story of Tom Brown at Rugby, however much a fiction, tells some wonderful facts in character education.

That every pupil's intellect is a part of his environment for good is apparent from what has been said above in reference to good habits and the conflict antecedent to their formation.

That every pupil has a different environment or total of influences is sure. One has a father, another has not; one has an Uncle Will, another has an Uncle Ben; one reads good books, another nothing; one is a prey to certain vices, another is free from them; one comes from a home where religion has sway, another knows nothing of it.

No two individuals are alike, because no two have the same environment.

Stupendous is the task upon the teacher of undertaking to train the characters of forty children, each having a different environment; great is his responsibility, but he should not shrink from the one or be appalled at the other. Much can be done by him in improving the environments of the several children in his charge; much can be done by him in educating their characters if he will but systematize his work.

The same postulates apply in educating the character, as are given in a former section to govern the teacher in training the intellect.*

In arranging his "wholes" for lessons in character a little reflection will show the teacher that they must be comprehensive enough to cover all grades of character-development in the class. That this is possible with any class will be apparent when one reflects that there is rarely very great dissimi-

---

*Postulate II will not be satisfied in a character-lesson unless the pupil's intellect, dominating his will, is one factor of his environment. He then becomes in truth "self-active;" *i. e.*, he completes the "whole" through which he makes a generic determination.

larity in their individual environments. These "wholes" must always be made up in part of material in the actual environment of the pupil, and the matter of them must be so presented as to cause each one to make a personal application of the matter presented to his own conduct; this is best done by a hypothetical talk, as will be illustrated later.

From what has been said above, the following principles for the guidance of the teacher may be inferred:

I. "Wholes" are identical only so far as their parts are the same.
II. A "whole" is made up of parts related.
III. Varying the parts varies the "whole."*

* * *

But a grave responsibility rests upon the teacher who constructs "wholes" to influence the life of a child. Wisdom has been defined to be, "The use of the best means for the attainment of the best ends." Whewell says, "We conceive *prudence* to be the virtue by which we select right means for given ends, while *wisdom* implies the selection of right ends as well as right means."

This being true, to guide his pupil to the highest ultimate ends the teacher must make his "wholes" serve as right means. A fourth principle then may be stated, as follows:

IV. The best interests of an individual are secured in the attainment of the best "wholes" possible.

An evident corollary of this principle is:

---

* One will not appreciate at a casual reading that these principles lie at the very foundation in character training. The lapse of time, the influence of the weather, the incidental influence of what has happened the same day, a thousand little influences that are potent in every "whole" presented by a teacher make it necessary to regard the truths asserted above at all times and in every lesson. One may attempt to do to-morrow or next year what he has successfully done to-day; but if he copies himself he will fail. The day, the hour, the pupils, and he himself are all changed elements in the "whole."

V. The best interests of his associates are the best interests of an individual.

* * *

The mind of man has three distinguishable yet not separable elements, viz., *Intellect, Emotion* (sensibility), and *Will*. These three in their functions are similar to the three Departments of our Government. Will is *Executive,* Emotion is *Legislative,* and Intellect *Judicial.*

The mind, through Emotion, by means of conscious resemblances and differences, discovers the *concrete* relations of sense-objects, and determines the Will.

The mind, through Intellect, by means of conscious resemblances and differences, discovers the *abstract* relations of sense-objects. It either approves or declares null and void the work of Emotion.

The Will, if it be a strong Executive, obeys the mandates of the Intellect; if it be weak or corrupt, it may fail in its duty.

This analysis of the functions of mind suggests two principles which are to the teacher alternatives:

VI. The teacher must provide a "whole" (environment subject to change) for his pupil, such that the concrete and abstract relations of the objects composing it will both act harmoniously in directing the will of the pupil.

Or, this being impracticable:

VII.* The teacher must try by hypothetical discourse to secure in the mind of the pupil a corresponding generic determination.

* * *

It must be evident to the reader that no one is able, in any

---

* It will hardly be possible, in any case, to so arrange a school as to keep evil influences out of a child's environment entirely, yet what can be done in this direction ought not to be neglected. Just so far as is practicable Principle VI should guide the teacher, but generally it will be found that Principle VII has also to be applied.

case calling for action in the now, to make a law for himself except from his past experiences.

The education of character consists largely in giving occasion for the most varied possible experiences on the part of the pupil. Hence the teacher must give to his pupil the most varied environments possible, or, as Postulate I requires, bring the pupil into as many and varied "wholes" as possible, and by repetition of such "wholes" secure assimilation of desired principles and consequent good habits.

These considerations are of sufficient importance to suggest another principle:

VIII. **The teacher must familiarize himself with the actual of his pupils, so that, as occasion offers, he may extend and vary their experiences.**

* * *

Now, as every good habit results from a triumph of the intellect over the emotional nature, and as every intellect will decide all cases according to what it thinks best for itself, and as the real best interests of an individual are generally found in sacrificing some of present pleasures, it becomes a difficult matter for the teacher to secure the formation of habits that are verily good. He must, therefore, take as his guide the truth expressed below, and by repetitions of "wholes," based upon *their* experiences, cause his pupils to assimilate and apply it by practicing self-sacrifice:

IX. **The future best interests of an individual require, in general, a present sacrifice of some pleasure.**

* * *

The teacher is one of the most important elements in the changing environments of his pupil. While all minds are alike in kind, probably no two are the same in degree. These differences in degree in minds tend to produce differences in kind in character. For these reasons another principle of the gravest importance presents itself:

X. The teacher must treat every pupil in accord with that pupil's character.

Rules should be as few as possible, and should be of that kind alone which are essential to secure unity and harmony in the conduct of the school. Also pupils should be taught practically to understand that no law applies to them as individuals until they have violated its requirements.

The tenth principle, indeed, calls for the very highest order of tact on the part of the teacher. If a pupil hears the bell which rings him to the class-room as a tyrannical command which is to be obeyed reluctantly, then that pupil is not entering into his " whole " freely; his is not a self-act; while he may enter the class-room and learn ever so much intellectually, he has not completed his "whole," and his character is not being educated; the teacher is failing with that pupil, and must continue to fail until in some way he can bring the pupil into a "better mind."

If, however, the pupil hears that bell as a clock ringing out the time of day when duty calls him to work, and goes gladly to his class, then he has entered into his " whole;" his character is being educated; the teacher is succeeding with him.

* * *

However much importance may be properly attached to the education of the mind, yet none the less importance must be attached to the healthful education of the body. It does not seem that a sound mind can coexist with an unsound body. A differentiation of functions for individuals or for classes in society which extends to the destruction of a healthful equilibrium of the physical structure or mental structure of the individual can not be conceived to be the best interests of society. Hence the principle:

XI. The teacher must ever attend to the healthful development of the body of the pupil.

* * *

An education which fails to give the body of the individual as an instrument into the possession of the mind is sadly out of joint with a healthful natural economy. A truly educated mind is ever using its body as an instrument in a struggle with the environment of the now. The present is the womb of the future. The dreamer of a future which is not founded on the present is the slave of his body. For such a being the final wreck of hope is certain. To destroy is not to establish. It is the pupil's mind, not the teacher's, which must control freely the body of the pupil. The tom-cat-like teacher of mice-like pupils can never educate the young correctly. Happy the pupil whose teacher can steer him clear of both the Scylla of license and the Charybdis of slavery in his education. Hence:

XII. The true teacher must ever have regard for the establishment of such an environment as will demand every day the exercise of the body as an instrument of the mind.*

* * *

It will be observed, on reflection, that in all correct teaching, in mathematics, language, and the like, the pupil is himself ever entering as a part of every "whole," and that hence in all proper education the character of the pupil is being educated. In an important sense assimilation means appropriation of the objective whole in a subjective state. The pupil who is so taught as to form the habit of obedience to assimilated principles in sciences is thus forming the habit of obedience to every principle of every kind.

Therefore:

---

*The truth announced in this principle is Nature's demand for the introduction of manual training into schools.

XIII. The end of all true teaching is the education of character.

DIFFERENTIATION IN CHARACTER.

Between boys and girls there are differences in character which become more marked when they become men and women. These are brought about by the promptings of *desires seeking ends*, thus giving birth to habits, good or bad.

As the ends apt to become constant, which are sought by the two sexes, are necessarily different, a difference in character is to be expected. But the difference is not so great as to make it inexpedient to educate the sexes together, as was once the rule.

However desirable it may be (and it would be better) to have separate schools for boys and girls, it has been found impracticable, and will probably remain so for some time, to have other than mixed schools for primary and secondary grades.

The general problem, then, of educating character must be complicated necessarily by the primal differentiation, male and female. What is said further, therefore, should be understood as drawn from resemblances and differences in conduct without reference to sex.

Character manifests itself in habits; and, as persons are observed to have *many* or *few* habits, so they need to be classified as to character according to these resemblances.

Active and *passive* are suggestive terms by which to characterize these two types of character, and will be used in this discussion to refer respectively to persons of many and of few habits.

Of persons who have developed or are developing *active* characters, some incline to contract good habits, while others heedlessly drift into bad habits.

Positive and *negative* are terms that will be used in this discussion to name characters as they may be differentiated by this observation.

EDUCATION OF CHARACTER.

Of persons who have few habits—passive in character—some are observed to tend toward the *positive*, others toward the *negative*, while a few can not be said to exhibit any tendency whatever.

These three classes of characters will be spoken of as *passive-positive*, *passive-negative*, and *typical-passive*.

For the convenience of the reader the full classification is here shown:

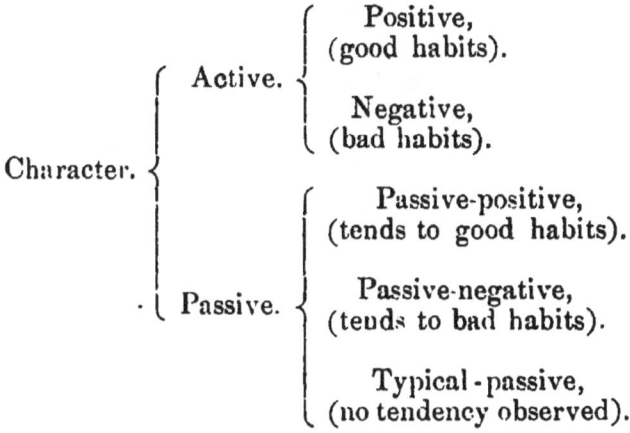

Somewhere in one of the classes named every boy or girl entering school finds his or her place. Each type of character demands an appropriate general manner of treatment. "To treat all alike" is a principle that defeats the end of educating character, whatever it may accomplish in securing good order and no complaints.

It follows, then, that a teacher, to succeed, must know his children, *i. e.*, know *their habits*, and apply the proper treatment to have habits continued if good, to change them if *bad*, and to induce habits if they are lacking.

If the child is *positive* in character, it is because he has had kind and wise treatment. Such good habits as he has acquired were born of his trying to make others happy, and have thus far been fostered by having his efforts appreciated.

As a rule, such children must be treated in school *exactly as they have been treated at home.*

This class of children bring apples to the teacher, or offer parts of their lunch to him, or volunteer to help him; if their little courtesies are not appreciated and recognized, they will gradually discontinue them, and be injured in character by the heedless behavior of the teacher.

If a child is *negative* in character, he has been treated unwisely at home. Too much has been done for him by his parents or elders; not cares enough have been put upon him; his selfish desires have been too much gratified; he has heard too much of the evil and too little of the good that he and others do; he has been lectured too much; or his efforts to do right (every child makes them) have not been observed and commended. This class of children are at "outs" with every thing that offers to restrain them in their desires; they enter school with feelings toward the teacher similar to those of a criminal toward his jailer.

The proper line of treatment for one of this class is to find out, first, how he *expects* you to do when he *tries* you, and then disappoint him by doing *some other* way. He must be made to experience pain for his misdeeds. Now, if he *expects* a whipping, he will take it and exult in his victory, because he has steeled himself to bear it; but if some other punishment is given it breaks him up.

Punishments ought to be in the nature of effects from causes. This makes them a part of the environment of a child, and hence they contribute to his education in right doing. But setting traps and watching them for victims is not the province of the teacher who wishes to educate character.

Negative characters need to be kept busy; cares must be put upon them; they must be brought into environments that will cause them in a natural way to desire to do right. They *expect* the teacher to watch them; hence he must *not* watch them. They have not been trusted by others; *he* must trust them.

Children who are *passive* in character are usually made so by actual cruelty; by repression of their activities, which amounts to cruelty; by being overtasked physically; by being allowed to indulge their appetites to excess, or by being allowed to contract unhealthy habits.

Such children are listless at play and inattentive at lessons; are slow and awkward in movement, and imitators of others in every thing; they are easily persuaded and easily influenced; negatives make cat's-paws of them.

The proper treatment of them consists (1) in making them *active*, and (2) in pursuing the line of treatment appropriate to the tendencies they may manifest.

"Making them active" can be accomplished, generally, through some study or play that will interest them. Try the whole range of things done at school till the pupil's natural bent is found. Give him free run in this pursuit until he has acquired independent action. By degrees he can be led to take interest, and become active in other studies or plays.

Drawing, modeling, and making things, if introduced into the regular curriculum, would save many a passive child that schools, as now organized, fail to interest and educate.

The foregoing analysis and remarks have been intended to assist the teacher as far as possible in systematizing his intercourse with those under his charge. If he will observe the habits of his pupils he can, in a few days, or weeks at most, classify them as: *Positive, negative, passive-positive, passive-negative,* and *typical-passive*.

This classification made, when a pupil tells you something, or asks a favor, or is observed to do a willful act, it assists in determining promptly what to do for his good.

A little boy, for illustration, tells you that Johnny has taken his ball. If both are *negatives*, you know at once that it was an act of reprisal. If Johnny is a *positive*, you know he has a claim on the ball that he thinks is good. If the boy who complains is a *positive* and Johnny is a *negative*, you know it is either a robbery or a case of plaguing. If Johnny is a *passive*, you should investigate the case fully in order to reclassify him. If the complainant is a *passive*, you know he needs protection.

No child is *positive* in every habit, neither is any one *negative* entirely. Care must be taken, therefore, to discriminate in every case that arises as to whether the parties concerned are *positive* or *negative* as to the *habit* involved in the case.

These suggestions have been made to guide the teacher in his every-day intercourse with his pupils. Much may be done in this way by a wise teacher, watchful of their welfare, to educate the characters of his pupils, but no one ought to be satisfied with this alone. Evil should be attacked and dislodged by regular approaches.

Children can be influenced by nature and law in the same way as their elders are. They are more susceptible, in fact, to good influences, because they have not become hardened in wrong-doing; because their passions have not become imperious by long indulgence, and because their intercourse with the world has not yet made them lose faith in promises not backed up by bonds, and does not yet incline them to regard every one who approaches them "bearing gifts" as a perfidious "Greek." The trustfulness and faith of children is great! Verily, he who is given charge of them has "talents of gold entrusted to his care," and it behooves him not to bury them in the earth as did the foolish servant, but to so use them as to return them, increased in value, to those who lent them.

When new words are met in the daily lessons whose meanings relate to ethical conduct, especial pains should be taken, as has been illustrated on page 53, that the learning of the new word be accompanied with the formation of a determination to act in accordance with the meaning assimilated.

HYPOTHETICAL DISCOURSE.

Moreover, at stated times, regular lessons should be given in the form of "talks" or conversations with the children about right behavior. At each of these lessons the teacher should make it the objective point to cause the children to assimilate some moral principle of wide application.

To insure assimilation of the principle and the consequent application of it by the children (see Postulate VIII, page 20,) in their conduct, it is absolutely necessary that there should have been *violations of it in deed or thought in their own experiences*, and that these violations should be brought to their memory by the "talk."

The bringing together of these facts of their experience, along with other facts brought into the discourse by the teacher, constitutes constructing a "whole" from which, through comparison, the principle desired may be assimilated.

This discourse, in its subject-matter, is apt to be largely hypothetical. It is never advisable to allude to the facts of their experiences, except as a supposition, or as things the teacher *once* knew to happen.

Any one may become expert in constructing a proper address to inculcate a lesson in conduct if he will but take the pains to collect the facts necessary, and remember that the law, *No one can learn a truth by reading it or hearing it unless he knows it already in its elements*, is never broken in the sphere of moral any more than in that of intellectual training.

A practical illustration is given below of a lesson from actual practice. The circumstances from which the *data* were derived, which served as the "elements known already" by the pupils, were as follows:

One Saturday in November the boys of a school organized a rabbit hunt. About twenty were engaged, and four rabbits were caught. Those who had caught the rabbits evidenced by their after-conduct an intention not to share the prey equitably. Certain directions were given to the cook by them as to how the rabbits were to be dressed, and to the table-boy as to where to set the dishes the next morning. The teacher had gathered all this in the course of the evening after the hunt. He said nothing to the boys at the time, and only interfered so far as to disturb the table arrangement the next morning. The rabbits were served from the head of the table along with the steak and other common dishes. Some surprise was apparent in the faces of a few, but no protests were made. The rabbit hunt and feast, in a few days, were no longer talked about.

Soon thereafter, at chapel exercises one morning, the following diagram was placed on the board by the teacher:

$$\text{Animals} \begin{cases} \text{men} \\ \text{not men} \end{cases} \text{co-operate} \begin{cases} \text{associate} \\ \text{herd}. \end{cases}$$

The habits of wolves and other animals were discussed by the teacher. The fact of their co-operation was brought out. Its general object, viz., to secure prey for eating, was dwelt upon. Their after-conduct, seizing and devouring each for himself, was exhibited. The fact that *no sharing* was a principle with wolves and other animals was made prominent. The end of their co-operation was shown to be in the securing of prey.

The conduct of men in co-operating was then taken up and compared with that of animals. A hunt of wolves had been elaborated, a supposed hunt of men was narrated in detail. Their conduct when prey was secured was contrasted with that of the wolves. Their motives in co-operating were examined, and the fact that their co-operating becomes permanent was emphasized, as also the fact that *sharing* is a principle with men.

Just enough was said in the discourse to insure the recall of the rabbit episode in the minds of the boys. No one was personally mentioned; no one was criticised; no one reproved.

The discourse accomplished the end intended, *i. e.*, it caused the *assimilation* of a principle by the boys, as was evidenced in a few days by remarks made in criticism of certain actions questioned about.

The lesson also incidentally served to classify properly the meanings of "associate" and "herd," as applied to actions of animals, the one being *permanent* and the other *temporary* co-operation.

R. D Allen, John T. Gaines

Pedagogics : A Monograph
A New Theory and Practice in Teaching

ISBN/EAN: 9783337167691

Printed in Europe, USA, Canada, Australia, Japan

Cover: Foto ©Paul-Georg Meister /pixelio.de

More available books at **www.hansebooks.com**

www.ingramcontent.com/pod-product-compliance
Lightning Source LLC
Chambersburg PA
CBHW020300090426
42735CB00009B/1157